FLOYD LITTLE'S TALES FROM THE BRONCOS SIDELINE

Floyd Little
with Tom Mackie

SP

SPORTS
PUBLISHING
L.L.C.

SportsPublishingLLC.com

Hardcover ISBN-10: 1-59670-050-5
Hardcover ISBN-13: 978-1-59670-050-5

Leather bound ISBN-10: 1-59670-183-8
Leather bound ISBN-13: 978-1-59670-183-0

Publishers: Peter L. Bannon and Joseph J. Bannon Sr.
Senior managing editor: Susan M. Moyer
Acquisitions editor: John Humenik
Developmental editor: Doug Hoepker
Art director: K. Jeffrey Higgerson
Dust jacket design: Heidi Norsen
Interior layout: Kathryn R. Holleman
Photo editor: Erin Linden-Levy

Sports Publishing L.L.C.
804 North Neil Street
Champaign, IL 61820
Phone: 1-877-424-2665
Fax: 217-363-2073
SportsPublishingLLC.com

Printed in the United States of America

CIP data available upon request.

To my three children and best friends—Marc Little, Christy Little Jones, and Kyra Little DaCosta; my three grandchildren, Skye, Blaze, and Hayes Jones, who will carry the torch for me in the next generation; and to my wife, DeBorah, who in addition to being the love of my life has become my great partner and friend.

—FL

To my wife Emily—your boundless heart made this all possible. And to my parents, Nellie Ray Mackie and James W. Mackie. This book is a testament to your everlasting love and support.

—TM

CONTENTS

FOREWORD

By John Elway

As a rookie with the Broncos in 1983, it didn't take long for me to learn about Floyd Little and his incredible impact on the Broncos organization. After all, Floyd retired in 1975 as the seventh all-time rusher in NFL history. More than that he was the Broncos' first superstar, a five-time Pro Bowler, a great humanitarian who immersed himself in charities on local and national levels, and the main reason the team was still called the "Denver Broncos," and not the "Birmingham Broncos" or the "Chicago Broncos."

In 1967 his signing as the franchise's first No. 1 draft pick finally squashed rumors that the team was relocating to another city. It started a love affair between the fans of Denver and the team's new star, contributing to the expansion of Mile High Stadium and years of sold-out Broncomania. As a result, Floyd aptly earned the nickname, "The Franchise."

On a personal level, I got to know Floyd shortly after my rookie season when he joined me and a number of Broncos on a cruise. I had a tough rookie campaign. He took the time to pull me aside and tell me to relax. He told me if I continued to work hard, good things would happen.

I continued to see Floyd each season when he played in my golf tournament. He became a successful Ford dealer in California and Washington, and that gave me the confidence that I could be successful when I started my own dealerships. We would sign memorabilia for each other for various charity events and send personal notes teasing each other about who was selling more cars. For all of Floyd's old-fashioned

Floyd Little and John Elway got to spend some quality time getting to know each other on this cruise following Elway's rookie year. Floyd is sandwiched in the middle (from left) with John, Keith Bishop, Steve Watson, and Dave Studdard.
Courtesy of Floyd Little

values concerning duty and responsibility, I learned he has quite a sense of humor, too.

Years later, after the Broncos finally got over the hump and beat the Green Bay Packers in Super Bowl XXXII, I couldn't help but fully appreciate the contributions of Broncos players from the past. I realized how much the championship meant to everyone. How it wasn't just a championship won by the 1997 Broncos, but a championship made possible by everyone who had ever worn a Broncos uniform. None stood out more to me than Floyd's contributions.

So I made a special effort to thank him when I saw him soon after that Super Bowl victory. "Floyd," I said, "because of you, the Broncos are

Super Bowl champions. If not for you laying the foundation so many years ago, this city never would have had a championship."

Floyd didn't say much. He didn't have to. I could see in his eyes that it meant the world to him. I was just happy to have the chance to tell him personally.

A couple years later in 2001 things went full circle for Floyd and me. I got to play with him and other Broncos in Mile High Stadium's Farewell Flag Football Game versus Joe Montana and the NFL Legends. Not only did we win the game, but I threw a touchdown pass to Floyd. That was surreal. You couldn't ask for a better ending, either. My son, Jack, then 12, got to hand off to Floyd on the game's final play.

As the only Denver Bronco to be in the Pro Football Hall of Fame, I am proud to be the first. But there are a lot of Broncos who deserve to be immortalized in Canton. Floyd Little leads that list and is long overdue.

Enjoy reading *Floyd Little's Tales from the Broncos Sideline.* You'll not only hear some funny stories about some of the greatest Broncos ever, you'll gain a clearer appreciation of Floyd's invaluable contribution to the Broncos organization. You'll learn why he's a legend of the game and, in my opinion, the greatest Bronco of them all.

PREFACE

By Jim Brown

When I came to Syracuse in 1953 there was no way of knowing that the No. 44 jersey given to me by Coach Ben Schwartzwalder would become legendary. As an African-American playing football in the 1950s, I faced many obstacles. I tried to adhere to my own code of excellence. I played the game with integrity and a dedication to be the best that I could. A couple years after I left for the NFL, another great runner, Ernie Davis, became the next great Syracuse player to wear No. 44. Ernie made a lasting impression on everyone who knew him. He was universally loved and admired. Ernie was a true gentleman who was as tough and determined as he was compassionate.

Ernie's competitive fire enabled him to become the first African-American to win the coveted Heisman Trophy in 1961. He also was part of Syracuse's lone national championship team in 1959. When he passed away in 1963 he became a part of our hearts and souls forever.

I didn't think anyone could match the impact that Ernie had left at Syracuse—until Floyd Little, who kept his promise to Ernie, became the next great runner to wear No. 44 at Syracuse. Floyd became the school's first three-time All-American. His toughness and zigzag style was uniquely his own. Floyd broke many records held by Ernie and me. Looking back, Floyd was the most productive of us all.

Floyd continued his greatness on the professional level with the Denver Broncos. Like me, he was picked sixth overall in the draft and watched as supposedly better running backs were rated ahead of him. The Broncos were never a great team, but Floyd proved to be a great running back. He became a highly regarded Pro Bowl player and respected

Floyd Little (right) poses with Jim Brown at a 2005 ceremony at Syracuse University to retire jersey No. 44, which both players wore while at the school.
Courtesy of Tom Mackie

captain. He gave his all for nine seasons, like I did. When he retired, he was the NFL's seventh all-time rusher.

For all his excellence as a runner, though, Floyd was an even better person off the field. His dedication and love for fans and teammates, his charitable work off the field, and his continued support for Syracuse University and the Denver Broncos continue today.

I've said for years that Floyd deserves to be in the Hall of Fame. There's no question in my mind that he's one of the game's greatest players. But he doesn't need the Hall of Fame's validation to secure his greatness. Just ask anyone who ever played with Floyd. They'll tell you he was a pro's pro and a true legend who probably did more for the team he played for, the Denver Broncos, than any single player in the league did for his own team.

1

HUMBLE BEGINNINGS

BORN TO RUN

From the first moment I can remember, I've been running. You could say that running was in my genes. I was the second youngest of six kids, and my three older sisters—Betty, Rosa, and Priscilla—were all fast runners. Betty was the oldest and the fastest of the bunch. She could run across town like she was riding on subway rails.

My father, Frederick Douglas, named after the famous abolitionist, died of cancer when I was six. That left my mother—Lula, a saint—to work several jobs to make ends meet. My mother was definitely the disciplinarian of the family, but Betty was responsible for raising me. I grew up in the projects in Waterbury, Connecticut. It was Betty I clung to. Literally. Wherever Betty went, I would hold onto her dress tail.

Back then women wore big hoop skirts, so I had a lot of fabric to work with. If I wanted to hang with her, I had to learn to run. People in the neighborhood would tell me, "You need to let go. Let your sister run and have some fun." My response: "No way." When I finally did let go of her dress at the end of the day, my fingers remained clenched, causing my hands to appear like claws.

Along with my sisters, I had an older brother, Fred. My father had nicknamed him "Ranger," because one of my dad's favorite radio shows was the *Lone Ranger*. My younger brother, Charles, was a serious guy who went on to serve in Viet Nam. While Charles became a decorated hero, Ranger was a bit of a troublemaker who often had run-ins with the law. It got so bad that we were forced to leave Waterbury. When I was 13, we moved to a small third-floor apartment in another ghetto in New Haven, Connecticut—not far from Yale University. Looking back, it was strange living in a poor section of an Ivy League town. Every day my family fought for survival, but not far down the road, it looked like the Gatsbys had moved in.

With money tight, everyone pulled their own weight in our family. We all worked. I started helping out when I was six, right after my father passed away. To earn some extra money for the family, I worked a variety of jobs, including shining shoes, delivering papers, washing cars, and working in a deli. I was always hustling. I think that work ethic at an early age made me a better athlete as I grew older.

HILLHOUSE DAYS

Early on I wanted to be a baseball player. I didn't really follow football until I moved to New Haven, and a buddy, Al "Tubby" Rogers, got me interested in playing the sport. I immediately fell in love with the contact. I had a lot of pent-up frustration as a kid, so football was a natural outlet. Kids saw how fast I was, and in pick-up games I was a receiver. I would run so far so fast that no quarterback could throw me the ball. Finally they put me at running back, and that's where I stayed.

My mother never wanted me to play football. I was small and she was afraid I'd get hurt. My sisters and I kept it a secret from her for years. Whenever I tore my clothes during a game, my sisters would sew them up without my mother's knowledge. We played on a rocky field with broken glass strewn across the ground, so my clothes were perpetually stained with blood. My sisters had a tough time keeping me looking like the Tide poster boy.

High school football coaches would come watch us play. One of them was Hillhouse High coach Dan Casey. I'd heard great things about

Hillhouse and was thrilled to go there. When I went out for the football team, I thought I'd be the starter. But I discovered early in my football career that life is all about overcoming obstacles. Not only was I not a starter, I was fourth string.

Our first home game was against Warren G. Harding high school. We were down 14-0 in the first quarter. So I went up and asked the coach to put me in. "Go sit down at the end of the bench," he yelled. I persisted. "Just one play," I begged. He shook his head in disbelief. By the second quarter both our first- and second-string backs were hurt and we were down 21-0. I knew if I could get in I could make a difference.

"Tell you what," the coach finally sighed, "go in and block and tell the quarterback to give it to [Bill] McCoy." Since I had just one play to make a lasting impression—I opted for a different message. I went in to the huddle and said, "Coach wants me to carry the ball." I took a pitchout and raced 68 yards for a touchdown. I handed the ball to the official and sat back down at the end of the bench.

Coach Casey walked over and told me to get back in there for the next series. "That's okay," I replied. "I just wanted one play." He was flabbergasted. When we got the ball back, he ordered me in. Again, I raced another 60-something yards for a touchdown. At this point, all of the other halfbacks were suddenly feeling better—ready to get back into the game. But it was too late. I scored five touchdowns that game and never sat the bench again.

BROTHERLY LOVE

My biggest inspiration during my early years came from my older brother, Ranger. I like to interpret it as "reverse psychology." Ranger was a troubled kid. Just two years older than I, he spent his days smoking, drinking, and hanging out with friends, often at Beaver Pond Park, the sandlot where I played sports every day. I would run around that park before every game to get fired up, while Ranger and his friends would sit on bleachers high as rockets and heckle me. "Why are you running so much, you ain't going anywhere," he'd say. "I can still whip your ass."

By 18, I could finally beat Ranger. It was then I decided to go all out all the time. I had three gears—fast, faster, and off-the-charts. I convinced myself to run as if I were stuck in third gear all of the time. Thanks to my brother's "reverse psychology," my determination to make something of my life was channeled into a boundless energy.

VALUABLE LESSON

When I began playing football, I was pretty confident. I didn't want to wear a lot of gear. Things like knee pads and thigh pads slowed me down too much. I also didn't think it was necessary to wear a jock strap. That is, until someone stepped right on my nuts in the middle of a pile. I had never felt pain like that. I was in pretty bad shape and had to be helped off the field. After that my jock was the first thing I put on. I even wore it in the shower. I never played without it again.

SCHOOL DAZE

After my first big varsity high school game, I didn't think anything could stop me. I made All-State as a junior and was eager for a spectacular senior season. But then I was informed that I was too old to play. I had been held back a year as a youngster because of an illness, and so I was a 19-year-old senior.

On top of that, my grades were poor. As a youngster, I mispronounced a word in school and was ridiculed badly by the other students. I refused to ever read aloud again, so I failed to become an adequate reader. Now that was coming back to haunt me. My guidance counselor told me to forget about college. I had hoped to get a football scholarship, but no school would take a chance on me. I even tried to get a job as a janitor, but I couldn't even fill out the application.

BORDENTOWN—NO MAN'S LAND

Bordentown Military Institute was a college prep school in Bordentown, New Jersey, not far from Trenton. Coach Casey apparently had written to Notre Dame and asked if they'd take a chance on me. Instead, Notre Dame suggested that he try enrolling me at Bordentown to get my grades up.

Here I am mugging for the camera in my uniform at Bordentown Military Institute, a college prep school in New Jersey that I attended for two years. As the first African-American to integrate the school, I had to grow up quickly. I learned discipline, responsibility, and a great deal of mental toughness. *Courtesy of Floyd Little*

The timing could not have been better. It was 1961 and BMI was one of many schools above the Mason-Dixon Line that didn't have any African-Americans. The headmaster at Bordentown, Dr. Harold Morrison Smith, wanted to integrate his school and thought I was mature enough to be the first African-American to enroll. He also knew I could help the football team. I had no second options, so the decision was an easy one. Before I knew it, I was heading to New Jersey, petrified to be the only black person at school.

NUMBER 77

It took me a while to get acclimated to Bordentown. The place was packed with military officers who were tough as dirt. I had to stand up straight, salute people, fire weapons, and take orders. I looked forward to football, but quickly found out that football at BMI was really boot camp with equipment. We did pushups, climbed rope, and crawled in the mud.

My coach at Bordentown was a tough son of a bitch named Al Verdel. He was like Vince Lombardi with an even worse haircut. I remember the first day of practice he gave me jersey number 77, to which I replied, "77? I'm a halfback, not a lineman." He stared at me like I had just pissed on his cornflakes. "Son," he whispered, "we run the Single Wing here. All backs wear numbers in the 70s. If you want to play, you'll wear this number."

From then on I thought wearing 77 was cool. That was Red Grange's number, after all. For people unfamiliar with the Single Wing, in it the quarterback is actually a blocking back. The halfback is the guy who takes the snap from center. I was happy to touch the ball on every play and we had a great team. We never lost in the two years I was there. In one season I scored 24 touchdowns in seven games.

Most of my teammates went on to become captains of their college teams: Joe Novogratz captained Temple; Joe Plumeri at William & Mary; and Phil Sheridan captained the 1965 Notre Dame team.

While at Bordentown, I turned enough heads on the football field to be offered 47 scholarships. *Courtesy of Floyd Little*

CLASHES WITH CLASSMATES

Becoming the first African-American at BMI proved to be a difficult transition. Most of my new teammates just stared at me, and very few said a word to me at first. My first roommate actually thought I grew a tail at midnight and turned into some kind of animal.

His imagination proved perfect for practical jokes. One night while he was sleeping I crept slowly up to his bed, sat at the edge, and yelled, "Aaaggghhh!!!" It scared the shit out of him. His eyes bugged out of his head and he howled like the world was coming to an end. "What the hell are you doing?" he screamed. "It's midnight," I said, "I want to show you my tail!"

It wasn't long before I had a new roommate, Herb Stecker. We both went on to Syracuse where he remained my roommate and was named co-captain with me during my senior year.

STRAWBERRY FIGHTS FOREVER

Just as I had done while at Hillhouse, I held several jobs at Bordentown. I needed the money to help cover my school expenses. One of my jobs found me working in the cafeteria. A guard on our team, Fred Jackson, worked there, too, and hated my guts. He was from Georgia, he didn't care for blacks, and he didn't take kindly to my efforts to be friendly toward him.

One day I was cleaning tables after dinner and there were a bunch of strawberry shortcakes left over from dinner that hadn't been touched. I put one on top of the refrigerator and dabbed some extra whip cream on it so I could identify it later when I went to eat it. At the end of the shift, I sat and ate my dessert, while Jackson just stared at me. The next morning he came up to me and said, "You switched desserts yesterday. You took my strawberry shortcake and ate it in front of me." I told him he was mistaken, but he didn't believe me. Jackson took my bowl of cornflakes and poured it on my uniform.

After weeks of this abuse, I lost it. I shouted, "Let's go." We went down to the train tracks and started swinging at each other. I had heard he was a boxer. So I waited for his best punch. He swung wildly and missed, and I floored him with a right hook.

At that point, six months of hostility just poured out of me. I started punching him so hard that I injured my hands. He had to be taken to the infirmary. We got in trouble and had to go meet the Commandant, Colonel Roosma. We walked into his office and the colonel got up and positioned himself inches from our faces. "I understand you had a fight without permission," he said. "Yes," we agreed. Back then, if you had a fight you had to actually sign something and have supervision. Obviously, we hadn't done that.

He gave us 100 demerits each. Then, right before he opened the door to excuse us, he asked, "Who won?" I had to bite my lip. Jackson's face was in poor shape; he looked like he had fallen off the top of an ugly tree and hit every branch on the way down. I didn't have a scratch on me. "Sir, I won," I said. And the commandant just nodded.

LIBRARY LUMPS

I got into another fight while working at the school library. One of my co-workers used to give me "Wet Willies," licking his finger and sticking it in my ear. He did it a hundred times before I finally flattened him. It wasn't the best decision, and I thought that was going to be it for me. I went back to my dorm room and started packing my bags.

Shortly thereafter, Col. Roosma knocked on my door. I let him in, and he lit into me, screaming for a good 10 minutes before I pushed him up against the wall. I told him, "It won't matter if I deck you. I'm already out of here." But he allowed me to tell my side of the story, and I think my intensity scared him. After he left I just sat on my bunk waiting for the military police to kick my ass out of school. By some miracle it didn't happen. I was confined to my quarters for the rest of the semester, except for practice and classes. But they let me stay in school.

When I came back for my second year at Bordentown, no one bothered me. I played football, but also basketball and track. While playing basketball, I was given number 44 for the first time. Little did I know it would soon become my favorite number.

PHOTOGRAPHIC MEMORY

While at Bordentown I had to take the SATs to be able to gain entrance into college. The first time I tested out at 210. You get 200 just for signing your name, so I thought, "This is crazy. I'm never going to suddenly become smart enough to pass." So I took an unusual approach to scoring well on the SAT: I learned how to memorize questions on the test, and then I learned the answers on my time. I concentrated on taking a mental picture of each question on the test.

The second time I took the SAT, I scored a 280—still awful, but I didn't give up. I joined a study group and hit the books every night for weeks. I went over each of the memorized questions with my professors until I knew the answers—a process that took weeks of studying. Luckily, the third time I took the test I was given the exact same test as my first try. I had memorized all the questions, and had memorized all the answers from my weeks of studying. My score went from a 280 to 1,200. I had finally passed with flying colors.

A year later, after I was already enrolled at Syracuse, I got called to the Dean's office. I walked in and a half-dozen administration people were waiting for me. They accused me of cheating on my SATs, claiming that someone else must have taken the test.

I was outraged. So I explained to them how I passed. They didn't believe me, of course, so I went so far as to recite for them the text of my test. "On page 58, the text reads . . ." I recited the page from memory, then did it for two more pages. The dean was dumbfounded. The faculty couldn't believe it. They immediately dropped the charges.

From that day on, my photographic memory served me well. I've been able to remember a lot of things because of this rare gift of taking mental pictures.

2

SYRACUSE:
The Legend of 44

RECRUITING WARS

The longer I was at Bordentown Military Institute, the more I started thinking about a military career. I thought the next logical step would be to enroll at Army at West Point. Many Bordentown graduates went to West Point, as well as Notre Dame and other fine schools.

One day Army's coach, Paul Dietzel, made a visit to Bordentown specifically to meet me. I spoke to our headmaster, Dr. Smith, about whether it was ethical to talk with coach Dietzel about going to Army when Notre Dame was the reason I was at Bordentown. Dr. Smith assured me that Notre Dame hadn't paid my way. "I'm the one who wanted you here," he told me. "No one else is responsible for you being here except me." That was the first time I had heard that, and it gave me such a feeling of independence.

A few weeks later I was invited to meet the man himself—Gen. Douglas MacArthur, the military legend. A limousine picked me up and drove me to Manhattan to the Waldorf Astoria Hotel. Gen. MacArthur had a suite there, and even though he was up in years he was as impressive as ever. When I walked through those doors it felt like I was meeting the president of the United States. Gen. MacArthur shook my hand and talked to me about the value of education and about being a leader. In addition to Gen. MacArthur, a slew of New York Yankees and Los Angeles Dodgers players were in the suite, and each of them were committed to getting me to go to Army. It was a veritable Who's Who of baseball: Elston Howard, Roy Campanella, Branch Rickey, and a few others.

I was told if I went to Army I could become the first black general. Gen. MacArthur told me how the military need more African-Americans. "There are opportunities," he told me, "to be a high-ranking officer." While the idea of being a role model for other minorities excited me, I wasn't unfamiliar with the recruiting game. They were telling me what they thought I wanted to hear, so I would go to Army and play football. But it was still impressive talk, regardless.

All told I had 47 football scholarships. Two years earlier I wasn't "college material," and now all these schools were after me. Due to the great influence that Army had on the coaches at Bordentown, and the tremendous impression that Gen. MacArthur left on me, I was leaning towards accepting Army's offer. But all that was put on hold after a snowy night in December, 1962.

MEETING THE INCOMPARABLE ERNIE DAVIS

I had just returned home to Connecticut after taking the Army's strenuous endurance test at West Point—to this day the most grueling physical test I ever took. I learned later that I had broken all the endurance records set by Army football legends Doc Blanchard and Glenn Davis, the original "Mr. Inside" and "Mr. Outside," who suited up in the mid-'40s.

I hadn't been home for more than an hour when the doorbell rang. A blanket of snow had covered the region, and the darkness of night was illuminated by light reflecting off the pristine snow. We opened the door and there stood four men, including a short, white gentleman with grey hair and glasses: Syracuse football coach Ben Schwartzwalder. The three

Meeting Ernie Davis—whose portrait I'm looking at in this photo—changed my life forever. Because of him and Jim Brown, I never forgot the honor and responsibility that came with wearing No. 44. *Courtesy of Syracuse University Archives*

men parted like Secret Service, and standing behind them was this tall, handsome man wearing a fine camel-haired coat. He was stacked up better than dirty laundry. It was Ernie Davis. My sisters were practically pawing at him through the door. "Who is that?" they kept whispering behind me. It was as if Elvis Presley was standing at our doorstep.

You couldn't imagine people like that coming to our rough neighborhood at that time of night. It seemed as if Ernie was their escort, not the other way around. The four men introduced themselves and invited me to dinner. I accepted, of course, and they took me to Jocko Sullivans, a fancy restaurant on the campus of Yale University. It wasn't every day that I was chauffeured to a fine restaurant, so I kept pinching myself to make sure it was real.

After we ordered, Ernie tapped me on the shoulder and said, "Let me talk to you for a minute." So I got up and followed him into the men's room. He put one foot up on the urinal and looked at me. I always wanted to be like Ernie, so I put one foot up on the urinal just like him as he began to talk. We looked like we were holding fort at the OK Corral. Our conversation lasted for about 45 minutes—right there in the men's room.

He told me, "I hear you're a real good football player with a lot of scholarship offers."

"Yes," I replied, "47 of them."

"Let me tell you a little bit about Syracuse," he continued.

I was all ears. I mean, here's Ernie Davis, the first African-American to win the Heisman Trophy, who had just signed a $100,000 contract with the Cleveland Browns, and another $100,000 endorsement deal with Pepsi. And here I was, cashing my checks at the 7-11.

"Coach Schwartzwalder likes to run the football," Ernie said. "His philosophy is three things happen when you pass, and two of them are bad. They can catch it, and you can drop it. Not good. At Syracuse you'll be running the ball.

"But more important, they care about your education. They want you to graduate. Even if you decide you don't want to play football anymore, you'll still keep your scholarship. That's one of the most important things about Syracuse University."

So I started thinking about all those scholarships I had been offered. They were *football* scholarships. This was more like an academic scholarship. My mother always wanted her children to get an education. Heck, she didn't even know I played football at BMI. So I replied, "Ernie, this sounds good. I'll go to Syracuse."

Even though Ernie's speech was impressive, I couldn't shake Notre Dame and Army from my mind. Months went by and I still hadn't picked a school. Then I received a phone call from someone during the spring who told me that Ernie Davis had passed away. I was shocked. I said, "Passed away? Ernie Davis, the Heisman Trophy winner? How could he die, he's only 23 years old?" The caller told me that Ernie had some rare blood disease called Leukemia.

I was trembling. "My God, I promised him I would go to Syracuse," I thought to myself. "How can I go back on a promise?" I hung up the phone and this incredible flow of emotion poured out of me. I couldn't believe such an amazing young man with such a bright future was gone— just like that. I decided that I owed Ernie my word. So I picked up the phone and called Ben Schwartzwalder. "Coach, I'm coming to Syracuse," I told him.

Ernie Davis had that kind of effect on so many people. I wanted to continue his fine legacy on the field, just as he had asked me to do. But more importantly, I wanted to aspire to be the kind of man he was off the field. He wanted me to wear No. 44 like he had worn, and Jim Brown before him.

THE LEGENDARY NO. 44

Even though Ernie Davis had promised me his No. 44 jersey, it wasn't guaranteed. Unlike today where freshman are eligible to play varsity, I spent my first year at Syracuse in 1963 playing on the freshman team. I must have made an impression on the coaching staff, because when I showed up at my first varsity practice in 1964, I was given No. 44. To wear the number and follow in the footsteps of the great Jim Brown, my idol growing up, and the incomparable Ernie Davis, well, it was beyond a dream come true. I instantly became part of history.

In 2005, during Syracuse's homecoming game against South Florida, Syracuse finally retired No. 44. It now sits in the rafters of the Carrier Dome. I was there for that unforgettable weekend, which culminated in the halftime retirement ceremony where Jim Brown, Ernie Davis' mother, Marie Fleming, and other great players, including Bill Schoonover, Michael Owens, Rob Konrad, and I were each given a replica No. 44 jersey and helmet from our playing days. My family and friends were there, including my grandson, Blaze Kennedy Jones, who I gave my jersey and helmet to. I've been told that the university may un-retire the jersey for special occasions. One of them will hopefully happen in 17 years when Blaze goes to Syracuse to play tailback for the Orange. He'll proudly wear his poppi's No. 44.

ANOTHER GUY NAMED FLOYD

My coach at Syracuse was a living legend. Floyd (Ben) Schwartzwalder coached the Orangemen from 1949-73 and went 153-93-3, won four Lambert Trophies and a national championship in 1959. But you'd never know it by meeting him. He grew up in the coal mines of West Virginia and had been a football star for the West Virginia Mountaineers in the 1930s. He joined the army in 1941 as a paratrooper and attained the rank of major. He also fought valiantly in World War II, fighting in many battles including D-Day while earning the Purple Heart, among other awards.

At only 5-foot-8, Ben didn't look like a former player or a decorated war hero. He was short, wore thick glasses, and spoke in a deep southern drawl. But he was one of the toughest guys I've ever known. He played center at West Virginia at the imposing weight of 148 pounds. He was an intense man who always clenched his fist and tightened his jaw when he spoke.

Unlike my coach at Bordentown, Ben wasn't a yeller. Instead he would pull you by the jersey and say, "C'mon, you're better than that." He was part psychologist, part father figure—a coach who was successful because of his football acumen and his interpersonal skills. He knew how to reach your heart, and he understood his players no matter their socioeconomic

Syracuse Coach Floyd (Ben) Schwartzwalder (left) was a tough, compassionate father figure. He also was a master motivator who fielded winning teams for 24 seasons—a true legend. Here I'm standing with him on the practice field.
Courtesy of Syracuse University

background. He treated us like family, always encouraging us in a positive way. He earned our trust and we ran through walls for him.

DIVINE ADVANTAGE

As a sophomore, I played my first varsity game against Boston College. I didn't start but played a little on both offense and defense. I knew right away that Division I football was a good deal tougher than anything I had faced before. BC beat us up pretty good, 21-14.

At the end of the game, the team chaplain, Father Charles, came up and put his arm on my shoulder and said, "Floyd, it's going to be okay. You're going to be okay." Now, BC is a Jesuit school. They have rows of priests sitting there at every game, and this one was no exception. I looked up at Father Charles and said, "I don't know, Father. Just look at all the priests they've got. We've only got you!"

KANSAS COMET MEETS THE KID

With one varsity game under my belt, I continued to work hard in practice. I was running with the second and third teams and often took plays the distance. Yet I never thought much of it since I wasn't with the first group.

We were playing Kansas that week and the whole nation was talking about their star, Gale Sayers. This guy was as smooth as Al Green and seemed to glide through the air when he ran. I was looking forward to the game. I kept thinking, "If they put me in on defense, maybe I'll get to tackle him."

I never got the chance. Minutes before the game started, Coach Schwartzwalder came up to Jim Nance, our powerful senior fullback, and said, "Jim, I'm starting you at fullback and the Kid at tailback." I sat there thinking, "Who's the Kid?" Then guys started tapping me on the shoulder saying, "Have a good game. Make No. 44 proud."

I was so nervous it reminded me of my first day at Bordentown. After an initial hit, though, I was totally focused. I scored five touchdowns on runs of 2, 3, 15, 19, and 55 yards, and totaled 159 yards on just 16 carries. We smoked them 38-8. After the game the first thing reporters asked me was, "Who are you?" I was just happy we won and I had performed well enough that people believed I deserved to wear No. 44.

GALE WINDS

I got to know Gale later that year when we both made the 1964 *Look* All-America Team. It was quite an honor since I was the only sophomore chosen. They held the banquet at the Waldorf Astoria Hotel in New York City, the same place where I had met Gen. MacArthur.

Gale and I went out on the town afterwards. He had just signed with the Bears and insisted on paying for dinner. We went to a bar and grill and had a good time. When it came time to pay, Gale took out this wad

Who are these two good-looking kids? That's Gale Sayers (left) and me at the *Look* All-America Banquet in New York 1965. As the only sophomore chosen, I looked up to Gale. We continued to bond after the banquet with an impromptu dash through the city. *Courtesy of Floyd Little*

of cash so big it looked like a head of lettuce. He had trouble folding it back into his pocket. I freaked out. My mom told me to never take money out in public, especially in New York. I only had a few bills on me, but I hid them all over my body: in my left sock, my right sock, inside my jacket, my pants pockets, behind my ears—everywhere but in my wallet.

"Gale, don't flash that money around. Someone is going to rob us," I warned. "Let's get back to the hotel right away." We both started looking around the room, and quickly paranoia crept over us. We left the bar so fast it looked like we were late for the subway. Once we hit the street we took off running. It dawned on me that two black guys running in the streets of New York at midnight probably didn't look too good to the cops. But before we knew it we were back at the hotel, laughing our asses off.

PENN STATE PINKOS

For decades Syracuse's archrival has been Penn State. Coach Schwartzwalder hated to lose to anyone, but he especially despised Penn State. In 1964, my first varsity year, we held our final team meeting the night before our game against Penn State. Five minutes into the meeting, Schwartzwalder stopped talking and started peering around the room. Then he began looking behind pictures and under the desk—for what, none of us knew. "Shhh, quiet everyone," he whispered. "This room is bugged. Follow me." He quickly ushered us down the hall to another room and immediately locked the door behind us.

"I have to tell you something," he said, looking serious as a judge. "People who go to Penn State are Communists. The coach, Rip Engle, is best friends with (Soviet Communist Party leader) Nikita Kruschev." We were like school children listening to tales of the big bad wolf. You have to remember, this wasn't that long after the Cuban Missile Crisis. The Communist scare was real, and Schwartzwalder had our attention. I was thinking, "Oh, boy, this is bad."

We were so scared that we went out the next day and had one of our best games of the season. I didn't want to be touched by a bunch of Communists, so I tried to score every time I touched the ball, and did on a 76-yard punt return with seconds left to seal a 21-14 win. In our 28-21 victory over Penn State during the following year, I scored three touchdowns, including one on a 91-yard punt return. Someone told me I even outran the film crew on that run. I tried to play that way all the time, but especially against Penn State.

Later when I was with the Broncos, I was invited back to speak at a Syracuse banquet. When I got up to the podium I looked out into the audience, and there in the front row was Rip Engle, the former Penn State coach. I wondered, "Oh, my God. What's he doing here?" I started to hyperventilate and kept glancing over at him. I was so nervous during my speech, and after I finished, I downed a full glass of water.

I played in the era of the tear-away jersey. Here I escape for a long gain my sophomore year against Holy Cross in 1964. On the ground laying a block is my first fullback, Jim Nance. *Courtesy of Floyd Little*

I pulled Ben aside. "Did you see him, Coach?" I asked anxiously.

"Who?" Coach wondered.

"Rip Engle!" I shouted. "What the hell is that Communist doing here?"

Well, Ben cracked this sheepish grin and looked down at the ground. "Floyd," he muttered, "Rip is, well . . . he's one of my best friends. He's not a Communist. I just made up that stuff to get you guys fired up. I guess it worked."

I was shocked. I laughed initially out of embarrassment. But boy, I was pissed. I was still very impressionable back then about the world, as were my teammates. We all fell for it.

DOGGONE SMELL

We used to joke that one of Ben's assistant coaches was his dog, who was often at his side. He had this big poodle named Casey that had a perpetual digestion problem. The dog would fart in meetings all the time.

While Ben gave his fire-and-brimstone pregame speeches, his dog would be stinking up the joint. Sometimes he ripped the silent but deadly kind. Other times the farts sounded like a clogged pipe fighting for air. Once in a while the dog seemed to time it so he let loose a doozey right at the end of Ben's speech—almost like an exclamation point for dramatic effect. The odd thing was the dog only seemed to do it while Ben was speaking, which didn't help our confidence in the game plan.

TECH KNOCKOUT

As an African-American player in the early 1960s, I experienced a fair share of prejudice. My first taste in Division I football came in a 1964 game versus Virginia Tech. Most of the southern schools had all-white teams, and Tech was no exception. But to the surprise of some, Tech apparently had no African-Americans in their entire school. Days before the game, one of our political science professors asked the African-American players to protest the game by not playing. I felt if anything, we would make a better statement by playing.

So we played and happened to win in the last minute, 20-15. I rushed for 155 yards and a touchdown, but it was a slugfest. Those guys beat the shit out of us. There was intense hitting on every play and plenty of pushing and shoving after the whistle. It was one of the most physical games of my college career, and the first time during a game in which I felt like someone hated me because of my skin color.

THE BIG UN-EASY

While the Virginia Tech experience lasted for just one game, the 1964 Sugar Bowl was a whole week of racial tension. We faced LSU, and even though Congress had just passed the Civil Rights Act, the country had a long way to go to achieve equality. Following my days at BMI I thought I was used to being judged differently. But that week in the Big Un-Easy—New Orleans, Louisiana—hurt me deeply.

There were only a handful of African-Americans on our team, so we pretty much stuck together when roaming around town. We tried to get a cab one night but none would stop. Finally, we saw a cab idling on a back street. We got in and the driver just sat there and read his newspaper. Finally, he looked up and said, "Don't you boys know this cab's for whites only? Get out!" We were infuriated.

Later, Charlie Brown—my teammate, an All-America defensive back, and an African-American—and I were walking down Canal Street and went into a Walgreens for a soda. Instead of serving us at the counter, the store clerk poured the soda in paper cups and told us we had to drink outside. Another store wouldn't even let us use the water fountain. Everywhere we turned we were judged by our color.

We practiced hard that week, and I thought we were going to run the ball down LSU's throat. But for some reason, right before the game Ben announced that our strategy was to surprise them by passing the ball. I ran the ball just eight times the entire game, and the strategy backfired terribly. We lost 13-10.

I don't know if it was the treatment some of us experienced that week, but we certainly didn't play with the same intensity that we had during the season. I felt emotionally drained by the time the game was over. The experience opened my eyes to the many injustices African-Americans were facing.

A RUN TO REMEMBER

By the time I finished my playing career at Syracuse I had broken many of Jim Brown and Ernie Davis' rushing records. I rushed for 2,704 yards and scored 46 touchdowns. Yet the thing I became most known for were my punt returns. I returned a record six punts for touchdowns, with three of those returns over 90 yards.

When it came to returning punts, coaches told me to never handle a punt beyond the 10-yard line. The problem was I always believed I could take it the distance, no matter how far it sailed. I know Coach Schartzwalder didn't always approve, but a few times it paid off.

One such time was against Pittsburgh at Shea Stadium in New York. It was my junior year, and the game had special meaning because my mother was there. I scored four touchdowns, including a 95-yard punt return. I found out later that New York Jets coach Weeb Ewbank and team owner Sonny Werblin both attended the game and were blown

My most memorable game at Syracuse happened during my junior year against Pitt at Shea Stadium. I scored four touchdowns, including a record 95-yard punt return. It meant more to me because my mom was there to share it.
Courtesy of Syracuse University

away by my performance. I was earning lots of looks from the NFL due to plays like that, which helped me become the nation's yardage leader with 199 yards per game.

Sometimes there are plays in your life that make such an impact that you can remember every cut, juke, slash, and dash. This was one of them. I can still hear coaches yelling at me to get away from it and let the ball go in the end zone. But I gambled and caught the ball at the 5-yard line. I started up field and dodged three players and cut back against the grain to the other side. It felt like crossing six lanes of traffic. Then I saw a tiny gap and dashed through the middle until the hole closed. I cut back to the right at midfield and noticed there were just two guys to beat. I turned on the afterburner and started eyeing the end zone. They had an angle on me, but I was able to gain some separation. I started thinking of how much I wanted to make my mother proud.

Somehow I was able to make it the final 50 yards for a wild 95-yard return. As I crossed the goal line I felt nauseated and dizzy. I turned around and there were guys strewn all over the field. The crowd was going bonkers, and I felt a great deal of pride—and relief. "Thank God Ben's not going to kill me," I thought to myself.

Afterward I sought my mother out in the stands and posed for a picture that appeared in the papers the next day. It's the one moment that stands out most during my Syracuse career because my mother was there to share it.

SECRET TO MY SUCCESS

One time Myron Cope, a terrific writer who later became the radio announcer for the Pittsburgh Steelers, asked me if there was a special ritual I performed before a game that allowed me to become so focused and intense during play. "Sure," I joked, "I drink a half glass of fresh blood on Saturday morning, sleep in a dark cage, and eat raw meat. Then when it is game time, I'm so excited to be free no one can catch me."

SPRAINED AND PAINED

Midway through my senior year in a game against Navy, my bright outlook changed when I severely sprained my ankle. Even though I was supposed to miss a few games, I had my ankle taped up and just played through the pain. Unfortunately, due to the injury I couldn't cut like before and my yardage plummeted. By the third game of the season fans started to boo me. They yelled, "What kind of All-American are you?" Some even called me at home to complain. I felt I had let the university down.

Aside from the injury, my weight dropped from 195 pounds to 183. I went for blood tests, but the doctor couldn't determine anything and instead just ordered more blood work. I was convinced I had leukemia like Ernie Davis. Finally, the doctor told me I had a massive iron deficiency. They started pumping me with vitamins, and my weight quickly returned to normal.

Still, I was depressed at my subpar performance and decided to quit. I made my way to Ben's office and told him of my decision. I was ready for him to tell me I was crazy to quit. Instead, he sat back in his chair with his chin on his chest, eyes looking at me above his glasses.

"Floyd," he began, "I understand if you want to quit. There won't be any shame in it. You have contributed more to the team than any player we've ever had. You don't owe this university a thing. But I want to tell you something. Of all the players I've coached, I think you're the best."

I became emotional, and the tears started flowing down my face. Ben wasn't the type to just throw out compliments. For him to say those things took me by surprise. "You've done enough for this university that you no longer need to play or come to games or anything. But I'd like you to stay at Syracuse, because I made a promise to your mother that I'd make sure you graduated. I'd like to keep that promise."

Then coach did something that to this day still opens the floodgates. Before I got up to leave he reached in his drawer and took out his paratrooper wings, the ones he earned parachuting on D-Day. He said, "I want you to have my wings. Please take them as a token of my appreciation for everything you've done at Syracuse."

My last home game for Syracuse was one of my best. We throttled Florida State 37-21 as I rushed for 193 yards and three touchdowns. And to think I was going to quit! *Courtesy of Floyd Little*

I was beyond speechless, a slobbering baby. I gave Ben a hug and practically crawled out of his office. I went back to my dorm and thought about the past four years. All the games, the All-America honors, being named captain, and the exhausting struggles I had endured. Then I thought about Coach Schwartzwalder and the man he was. I thought about my teammates and how proud I was to be a part of the tradition at Syracuse. My thoughts turned to finishing up the season with the team, and then seeing what the future might bring.

There was just one home game left against Florida State, and we were fighting for a bowl berth. I went into Ben's office and told him I wanted to play. He looked at me for a few seconds then said, "Go suit up." I went out and had one of the best days of my career. I rushed for 193 yards, scored three touchdowns, and helped defeat the Seminoles 37-21.

I had enjoyed bigger days before that, like my 196 yards and four touchdowns against West Virginia. But this meant more. As I jogged off the field at Archibold Stadium for the final time I saw a bed sheet draped over the visiting locker-room entrance. It read, "Booth III thanks Floyd Little." Booth III was my freshman dormitory. That simple tableau almost dropped me to my knees. To know that guys from my freshman year of school wanted to pay tribute to me in my last home game was an incredible ending to a memorable career and a difficult few weeks.

To this day, I get choked up thinking about that day in Ben's office. Those wings meant so much to him. But then I have to laugh. I mean, Ben was a master motivator. Part of me believes he had a box of those wings in his desk that he handed out to players whenever they felt like quitting!

LARRY CSONKA

After Jim Nance left for the pros, Larry Csonka became my fullback during my junior and senior years. Of course, everyone knows about Larry's exploits in the NFL; he was the immovable force of those great Miami Super Bowl teams in the 1970s. Larry was one of those naturally strong guys. He grew up on a farm in Ohio and had the biggest arms, shoulders, and head you ever saw. His helmet was the size of a milk bucket, and he also had a big butt. Whenever we ran out of the I formation, all I could see was Larry's ass. He was so big that opponents couldn't always see me running behind Larry. Then again, I could never see what was going on in front of him.

Our offense was pretty simple. We ran an unbalanced line with four linemen on one side and two on the other. Our All-America tackle, Gary Bugenhagen, was usually the lead guy. We'd break the huddle and opponents would yell, "Run, run!" even if it was third-and-forever.

Before we'd get down in our stances, Larry would ask, "Floyd, who do I have?"

"No. 68," I would respond.

And he'd say, "That guy?" and point right at him. The defender, realizing the play was going right over him, would mutter, "Oh shit!" under his breath.

Larry probably doesn't know this, but I'm the guy who got Ben to switch him to fullback. When our starting fullback, Ron Oyer, went down in '65, Ben said, "What are we going to do, we have no fullback?" I suggested moving Larry from linebacker to fullback: "How about Pigeon?", which was Larry's nickname because he walked with his knees knocking like a pigeon. "I'll tell him what to do until he learns the plays." Well, the first few games Larry mostly blocked, only carrying the ball maybe three times. But after he became comfortable, he wanted to carry the ball more. I wasn't really in favor of that because that meant I was in front of him doing the blocking!

Larry and I got along great. I was a serious guy, even in college. Larry was more laidback. He watched the way I handled myself and told me later that he had decided if he wanted to make it to the pros he'd better start mirroring his life after mine and become more dedicated. Of course, we shared plenty of jokes, too. He used to tell me, "Floyd, if I didn't like you, I'd fart in your face before every play." Good thing he liked me.

TOM COUGHLIN

If you ask me, one of the better sports trivia questions out there is: "Which current NFL coach played in the same backfield with Larry Csonka and Floyd Little?"

The answer is Giants coach Tom Coughlin. Tom was our wingback my senior year. Knowing his reputation now as a strict disciplinarian, people often ask, "What was Tom like as a player?" All I can say is that Tom was a big pain in my ass. He was a mister know-it-all; but not in a really bad way. He got on the nerves of a few guys because he not only knew all the plays, he also memorized all the assignments of every player. If quarterback Rick Cassata called a play in the huddle and he mispronounced it or called the wrong formation, Tom would correct him. And if someone was unclear on an assignment, Tom wouldn't hesitate to tell them what they needed to do.

Tom wasn't the most talented player, but he worked incredibly hard. He was the first one to meetings and practice—always early, I might add—and the last to leave. He really wanted to carry the ball, but there was little chance of that happening with Larry and me back there. We'd

Syracuse's 1966 backfield was stacked: (left to right) quarterback Rick Cassata (23), me, wingback and future NFL coach Tom Coughlin, and my man, Larry Csonka. *Courtesy of Syracuse University*

tease him, "Tom, you're never going to carry the ball as long as we're here. Get used to it." There was one play, however, that did call for Tom to run the ball. The play was called "Syracuse Scissors" or "44 Scissors." Basically, it called for the wingback to line up outside the tight end and take an inside handoff toward the line while the rest faked a sweep. Tom loved that play and ran it well in practice.

But on game day, Ben would call for me to carry it instead of Tom. The play would come in and Rick would say, "44 Scissors Play," and Tom's eyes would light up. Then he'd add "tailback switch." And poor Tommy would be crestfallen. I felt bad for him, but damn I loved that play. Jim Brown and Ernie Davis ran it to perfection. So naturally I got to run it. It was a great misdirection play. If you hit the hole just right, you had only the safety to beat.

It's not surprising to me that Tom became a fine coach. There are players who don't like his style, but Tom was an overachiever as a player and wants guys to be the best they can be. His intentions are honorable. You always hear there's no substitute for hard work. Tom is the patron saint of hard work. Just look at the difference in the Giants his first year when he tried to instill some discipline, and this past season when players finally bought into his methods. They went from 6-10 to 11-5 and winners of the division crown.

If I were coaching, I'd be even more of a disciplinarian than Tom, in the mold of Vince Lombardi. I'd say, "We're going to do it this way, and if you can't do it, then get the hell out of here!" Lucky for this generation of players, I went into the auto business.

216 YARDS NOT ENOUGH

We played Tennessee in the 1966 Gator Bowl in my last game for Syracuse. This time Ben assured us that we would be running the ball— a lot. Larry and I had developed into a solid one-two punch.

We were determined to win and approached the game very seriously. Tennessee had a very good team, featuring a solid defense that held teams to less than 10 points a game. Even though we ran well against the Vols, we found ourselves down 18-0 at halftime. Tennessee's passing game was killing us. Larry and I scored in the second half to make it 18-12. But when we got down close to the goal line near the end of the game, Ben called for Oley Allen to carry the ball. Oley fumbled and we were finished.

I was devastated by the loss. It wasn't just Oley's fumble. We had several turnovers and failed to capitalize in some key situations. When a team compiles over 350 yards rushing and loses, something is wrong. I left everything on the field, rushing for 216 yards—my highest total ever. Larry added another 100-plus yards. My jersey was so shredded it looked like a soiled rag.

After the game a teammate, Joseph Radivoy, asked for it as a memento. I said, "Sure," and handed him the jersey. I never thought about it again. Then last fall at the No. 44 retirement ceremony, Joe told me he still had the jersey and wanted to give it back. He mailed it to my oldest daughter, Christy, and when she got it she called me crying. She said it still had the grass stains on it and had been well preserved in a plastic bag. I was amazed. I thought, "Boy, I bet it smells pretty bad!"

THREE TIMES A CHARM

I really enjoyed my time at Syracuse. Everything I attained later in life really started with my success in college. I met an attractive girl, Joyce Green, whom I married and had two beautiful daughters with. When we went out we usually went to The Varsity, a fabulous eatery where Jim Brown and Ernie Davis used to hang out. It's still there like it's been for over 50 years. Whenever I go back to Syracuse, I always stop by The Varsity—especially since they refuse to allow me to pay! On my trips back to Syracuse I've met many current student athletes, as well as other Syracuse alumni who have carried on the tradition: Art Monk, a deserving future hall of famer, Joe Morris, Rob Konrad, and youngsters like Marvin Harrison, Donovan McNabb, and Dwight Freeney.

Perhaps the thing I'm most proud of from those days is that we always had a winning team. We upheld the standard that Ben Schwartzwalder established when he arrived in 1949. I loved my teammates because they never gave up in any game. Their dedication and commitment were instrumental in my success. I am grateful for everything they did to help me become the player I developed into. Because of them, I became college football's first three-time All-American since Doak Walker and a top candidate for the Heisman Trophy each year. My college teammates and I have gotten together numerous times over the years and enjoy sharing old stories and reliving all those games. They are a tremendous group of guys who respect me, just as I do them.

3

WELCOME TO THE BRONCOS

PRE-DRAFT RUMORS

The 1967 NFL Draft was unique because of the impending merger between the AFL and the NFL. The AFL had become a very popular league. It was a wide-open league that starred exciting players like quarterback Joe Namath of the Jets and Lance Alworth of the Chargers. It wasn't a three-yards-and-a-cloud-of-dust league like some people viewed the NFL. Before Namath signed that incredible $400,000 contract in 1965, the AFL usually missed out on the top college players. Players were drafted by an NFL and AFL team, and then a bidding war would ensue to see who could offer the most money. Since the AFL didn't have the money or the prestige, 99 times out of 100 the top players jumped to the NFL.

That all changed the year I was drafted in '67. For the first time the draft operated a "common draft," like it does today. Only one team could draft you and that team had first rights to sign you. With no bidding war to fall back on, the players selected in the '67 draft were not going to strike it rich like Namath. Still, I was told by Jets coach Weeb Ewbank and owner Sonny Werblin that I was going to be Joe's teammate. They had been at Shea Stadium to watch my four-touchdown game against Pittsburgh in 1965 and told everyone, "He's the best. We want him." It was exciting to think about playing for one of the AFL's brightest teams—especially since it was close to Syracuse and my family in Connecticut.

I felt pretty good about my future. Then right before the draft, an article appeared in *Sports Illustrated* that all but rejected me as a top pro prospect. As so-called experts, I suppose the authors felt the need to set the record straight. One concern was my age. At 25, I was ancient for a running back. Then there was my size, or lack of it: 5-foot-10, and 195 pounds. They said I was too small. I remember a reporter teasing me, "You're just a 'Little' guy, aren't you?" He seemed amused by his bad pun as if he was the first guy to ever tell me that. I replied, "My heart is as big as any man out there."

Most backs in the NFL were 6-foot-2, and 215 pounds. So they ranked me behind bigger prospects like Michigan State's Clint Jones, UCLA's Mel Farr, Texas Southern's Willie Ellison, Arkansas' Harry Jones, and Idaho's Ray McDonald. They all had about four inches and 20 pounds on me.

I took the criticism personally. "How dare they tell me what I can or cannot do," I thought. "I'll show them. I'll go to the Jets with the 12th pick and enjoy a great career in the country's biggest market." Deep down, though, I started thinking that if pro teams seriously bought into the article then I might still be around in the last round. My sophomore year Wake Forest's Brian Piccolo led the nation in rushing and scoring and went undrafted. And he was bigger than me.

THE BIG DAY

The first few picks of the draft were predictable. Bubba Smith, Michigan State's mammoth defensive end was chosen first overall by the Baltimore Colts. How Baltimore, an elite team, ended up with the top pick, I still scratch my head over. But, I guess, they must have traded with someone. The Vikings selected Michigan State running back Clint Jones next. Then two quarterbacks were taken: Heisman Trophy winner Steve Spurrier from Florida went to the 49ers, and Purdue's Bob Griese went to the Dolphins. With the fifth pick the Houston Oilers chose linebacker George Webster, yet another Spartan!

Now the Denver Broncos were on the clock with the sixth pick. The draft wasn't televised, so the players simply sat by the phone waiting for the call. There were 17 rounds, so a guy could burn through a few pairs of pants just waiting. I was still hoping that the Jets would choose me, but I'd also spoken to the great Vince Lombardi about the Packers, who held the ninth pick. Little did I know something was brewing in Denver that would forever change my life.

The Broncos had made it clear among their brass that they were drafting Gene Upshaw from Texas A & I, now known as Texas A&M-Kingsville. But right before their pick, coach Lou Saban turned to Broncos Public Relations Director Val Pinchbeck, who just happened to be Syracuse's former PR man, and asked, "Val, what kind of player is Floyd Little?"

"Why, Floyd is a great player," Val said. "He's a consensus All-American and a terrific runner."

Then Lou asked, "What kind of person is he? Is he someone you can build a team around?"

Val nodded, "Absolutely. Floyd is a great person. He was captain and an outstanding leader." Lou stood silently for a moment. Val continued, "Why are you asking? You said you're drafting Upshaw."

Lou looked back and smiled, "We're not drafting Gene Upshaw. We're going to draft Floyd Little."

When the phone rang, I expected to hear Coach Ewbank's voice on the other end. Instead I heard the booming voice of Lou Saban. "Floyd," he said, "this is coach Lou Saban. Welcome to the Denver Broncos."

And that's how I became a Bronco.

WHERE THE HECK IS DENVER?

My first reaction to being drafted by the Broncos was shock. I wasn't even sure where Denver was on the map. I was an Easterner and thought it was some cow town in the middle of nowhere. And because I had never heard of the Broncos, I thought, "Maybe they're not very good."

I checked their record and I was right. Denver had been one of the AFL's worst teams for years. They had never had a winning record in the franchise's seven-year history, and often they ended up in last place. They had a couple of good players—receiver Lionel Taylor and defensive back Austin "Goose" Gonsoulin—but by the time I got there, they were both gone.

People had made fun of their uniforms for years. Their "barnyard brown" colors were accented by vertically striped socks that were hideous and had become a running joke among sportswriters. Later when they switched to orange and blue uniforms, the media made fun of the funny orange helmets with a cartoon horse that looked like a giant inkblot.

The first thing I thought was, "I'm not going to last too long there. I'll get killed." I headed out to Denver with my agent, Andy Marciano, expecting the worst. Instead I fell in love with the place. It was a friendly town surrounded by the most beautiful mountains I've ever seen. Most of all, I really liked Coach Saban. He was a no-nonsense guy who had coached the Buffalo Bills to back-to-back AFL Championships a couple years earlier, before going back to the college ranks to coach the University of Maryland for a year, a school that Syracuse played often.

"We're going to build a team around you," Lou told me in our first meeting. That made me feel welcome. I was excited to be thought of as the foundation for a franchise on the rise. But the truth was ugly. The Broncos organization was in disarray, and the owners—Gerald and Allan Phipps—had threatened to move the team several times to Atlanta and Chicago. Now they were intent on moving the Broncos to Birmingham, Alabama. I wasn't too keen on the South at that point, remembering my Sugar Bowl experience in New Orleans, so I was hoping we stayed in Denver.

The point of contention was the Broncos' stadium. At the time, Denver played in an old minor league baseball park called Bears Stadium. It looked like a giant erector set. One of the requirements of the AFL-NFL merger was that each team's stadium had to seat at least 50,000 people. Bears Stadium probably seated half that number. And just before I got there, a $250,000 stadium bond that would be used to upgrade the stadium was rejected by the folks of Denver.

The biggest surprise of my life was being drafted by the Denver Broncos in 1967. As an east-coast kid, I had no idea where Denver was and had never been on a horse for that matter. Still, I quickly fell in love with the city and the fans.
Courtesy of the Denver Broncos

As the first No. 1 pick to sign with Denver, I was looked upon as the savior. The franchise was rumored to be moving to a number of cities. But as the "new" Broncos we traveled all over Colorado and beyond to generate support for the team. It worked. The Broncos never packed their bags. *Courtesy of the Denver Broncos*

The Broncos were headed to Alabama unless something drastic happened soon. Ownership felt that the first step to keeping the team in Denver was to sign their top pick—me. The Broncos had never signed their No. 1 pick before. In the past they had drafted future Hall of Famers—Merlin Olsen, Dick Butkus, Paul Krause, and Bob Brown— plus great pros like Bob Hayes, Ray Mansfield, and Marv Fleming. But each of them scoffed at playing for Denver and high-tailed it to the NFL.

So I waited for Steve Spurrier to sign with the 49ers and then asked for 50 cents more. Seriously. I just wanted to make a few pennies more than the Heisman Trophy winner! The combination of my signing and the addition of a great coach like Lou Saban began to pique the interest of Broncos fans.

Still, the city needed to raise about $2 million to keep the Broncos in Denver. A group of Broncos supporters helped raise the necessary funds. Corporations started donating money, the Phipps matched the contributions, and we players went door to door to raise more money. We rode in motorcades with the tops down so fans could meet us. We walked down crowded streets shaking hands. We hopped on buses and made goodwill trips throughout Colorado, Wyoming, Nebraska, the Dakotas—all over Broncoland.

The results were amazing. A true grassroots effort to keep the city's beloved Broncos in Denver was underway. I was already being recognized as a savior without having ever played an NFL game. People were buying up tickets because I was the first No. 1 pick to sign. The team's PR staff coined us "The *New* Broncos." But without all of our fundraising efforts, we would have been the new *Birmingham* Broncos. Finally, the money was raised and the stadium began undergoing expansion. When finished a few years later, the name was changed to Mile High Stadium.

I had become part of something special in a town that was unknown to me just a few months earlier.

COLLEGE ALL-STARS

I began my professional career playing in a number of All-Star games. The first game, you could say, offered a bit of a challenge. I played against the world champion Green Bay Packers in the annual College All-Star game in Chicago. Up until 1976, before high salaries and the fear of injuries halted the contest, the top college seniors played an annual exhibition game against the NFL champions. The Packers had just walloped the Kansas City Chiefs 35-10 in Super Bowl I. It was up to us baby-faced college kids to take them down.

During the All-Star week I got to meet a number of fellow rookies and new Broncos teammates: guard George Goeddeke and defensive tackle Pete Duranko from Notre Dame; Mike Current from Ohio State; and tight end Tom Beer, from Houston. I also got to know the guy who the Broncos initially wanted to draft—Gene Upshaw, who became a Raider. We got along great, and Gene gave me the nickname "Wheels," because, he said, my bowlegs were round like wheels. Over the next nine years

Gene and I would face each other many times in those Broncos-Raiders games. To this day, even as the executive director of the NFL Players Association, Gene still calls me Wheels.

We "All-Stars" lost 27-0 to the Packers, but the score might as well hove been 127-0. All I remember is getting my ass handed to me on every play. Our quarterbacks were Steve Spurrier and Bob Griese, and all of us were being tossed around like pint-sized rodeo clowns. I learned very quickly that the NFL was full of great players. I also realized why the Packers kept calling us "All-Stars," because that's all my aching head could see—stars.

THESE SPIKES ARE MADE FOR WALKIN'

While I was away playing in the All-Star games, the Broncos made history by becoming the first AFL team to beat an NFL team. It was an exhibition game in Denver against the Detroit Lions. During the coin flip, Lions defensive tackle Alex Karras looked around the stadium and said to our defensive end, Dave Costa, "If we lose, I'll walk to Detroit." We took a 10-0 lead early and beat the Lions 13-7. Almost 40 years later, I guess Alex is finally crawling up his driveway.

NFL, MEET MR. GILCHRIST

The next week we beat another NFL team, the Minnesota Vikings. I started at tailback with the great Cookie Gilchrist at fullback. Carlton "Cookie" Gilchrist was an awesome specimen. He was the first to gain 1,000 yards in the AFL and was the league MVP in 1962. As big as Jim Nance and Larry Csonka were, Cookie was even bigger. He stood 6-foot-3 and was listed at 250 pounds. But I'm telling you, he was more like 270. He was all muscle, too. I heard he once got into a fight with then-heavyweight champion Sonny Liston over a woman and whooped Sonny's ass.

Before I met Cookie I considered myself a pretty tough guy. But he was the toughest football player I knew. He didn't think much about his appearance when he was on the field, which made him even more intimidating. Sometimes he didn't wear a jockstrap or chinstrap in games.

In practice he wore street socks. It was almost like he crawled out of bed, grabbed his helmet, and calmly went about the business of kicking someone's ass each day.

A few years earlier Cookie had played on Lou Saban's back-to-back AFL championship Bills teams before going to Denver and Miami. Now, in the last year of his career, he was back with the Broncos. But, boy, he could still play. We ran a lot of sweeps that day and Cookie just destroyed the Vikings' two defensive ends, Jim Marshall and a rookie named Alan Page. By halftime, Page, now a Hall of Famer and a Supreme Court judge in Minnesota, was moved inside to defensive tackle, where he remained the rest of his career.

Cookie and I each scored touchdowns in that game, and we beat the Vikings 14-3.

RAIDER HATERS

A week after that Vikings game, we flew to Nebraska for my first away game as a professional. Nebraska was celebrating its centennial, so the AFL decided to host a game there between the Broncos and Raiders. I guess the organizers wanted two teams that hated each other—and they did a good job in picking us.

We won 21-17, and Cookie dominated another defensive end, big Ben Davidson. Davidson was afraid of Cookie. Every time we ran a sweep, Cookie buried him. After a half-dozen sweeps, Davidson looked like he was just trying to get out of Cookie's way. Cookie taught me a lot about not being afraid of anyone and never backing down. I was lucky and honored to have played with him.

Besides Cookie's performance on the field that day, the thing I remember most about that game was our plane flight out of Nebraska. We were in a small plane, and after take off I noticed we were circling the airport, slowly trying to rise higher with each go round. Finally, the pilot spoke to us over the intercom to explain what was going on. He told us that due to the weight of the passengers, the plane was trying to gain momentum to pull itself over the Rocky Mountains.

For someone like me, afraid of flying, this did not bode well. I was looking around for a few guys to throw off the plane to make it lighter.

After we got over the mountains, the pilot asked for the bigger players to move to the front to keep the nose down. I started thinking, "Yup, the AFL definitely is the poorer league."

4

THE LOU SABAN YEARS:
The Man and the Mayhem

ONE INTENSE COACH

You've probably seen clips of Lou Saban on NFL Films uttering an intense, memorable sound bite. I can assure you that he wasn't just mugging for the camera. That was Lou. He hated losing, despised mistakes, and would get so caught up in a moment, he would fire you and everyone associated with you for the smallest of problems. If the sun cast a wrong shadow on you, you could expect a pink slip hanging in your locker. Coach Saban could be warm, caring, and soft-spoken, too, but the next minute he could turn into the Tasmanian Devil.

I remember Lou fired our receivers coach, Sam Rutigliano, who later became the Browns coach, during Sam's first game with the Broncos. Sam was up in the press box on the phone with Lou during a crucial fourth-down play. There was a miscommunication and the play failed. Lou yelled up to Sam that he was fired and should go pack his bags. The rest of the game Sam wondered what he was going to tell his wife since they had just arrived in Denver and had barely unpacked their belongings. We came back to win the game, 26-21, and afterward Lou pretended it never happened.

Lou was the epitome of the irrational and irascible football coach. He had been a heck of a football player for the Cleveland Browns back in the 1940s with Coach Paul Brown and quarterback Otto Graham. They were part of the All-American Football Conference then, which later merged with NFL. During the four years that Lou played linebacker and fullback, the Browns won the AAFC Championship each year. After his playing days, Lou went into coaching and had great success, winning those two AFL crowns with the Bills. So, like me, he wasn't accustomed to losing.

PULLING A SABAN

You recall the 1999 NFL Draft when "Iron Mike" Ditka, then the Saints coach, traded all his draft picks so he could move up to nab Texas running back Ricky Williams, the Heisman winner. Since that time, when an NFL team makes a bad deal critics refer to it as "pulling a Ditka." But I like to think of it as "pulling a Saban."

In 1967, my first year with the Broncos, Lou decided we needed a top-flight quarterback. Evidently Lou wasn't impressed with the Broncos' stable of quarterbacks from the year before, that had combined to throw 30 interceptions and just 12 touchdown passes. He had promised to build a team around me, and so I thought he was going to either draft a great quarterback or make a trade for a proven veteran. He did neither. Instead, he jeopardized the Broncos' future by giving away two first-round draft picks—our 1968 and '69 picks—for Steve Tensi, a Chargers backup quarterback. Steve had attempted only 52 passes in his short career.

Still, we all gave Steve the benefit of the doubt. He was tall (about 6-foot-5), rail thin, and had long sideburns. He often slicked back his hair and loved to sing Elvis tunes. He also was a bit of a ladies man, and so I wondered if he actually thought he *was* the King. Well, this Elvis must have sung a lot of blues, because he got hurt often. Our pass protection was abysmal during those early years and our quarterbacks got smacked around a lot. Now, I liked Steve—he had a good arm and was pretty tough. Everyone agreed, though, that he wasn't worth those two No. 1 picks. By 1970, bruised and battered, Steve had hung 'em up.

Lou Saban was the epitome of an old school football coach—tough, demanding, and easily irritable. Football was his life and we loved him for it.
Courtesy of the Denver Broncos

ROOKIE ROUNDUP

Twenty-six rookies made the team in 1967, my first season with the Broncos. That's not a misprint. I still think that must be an NFL record. But it didn't phase Lou, who liked to bring in new kids all the time. On several occasions, I was at my locker changing into my uniform and the guy at the locker next to me was someone new whom I had never seen before. Often, by the following day, the guy would be gone and someone else would be in his place.

One time we actually signed a guard an hour before the game. I didn't meet him until we were in the huddle. Someone introduced us before our first play: "No. 62, meet Floyd Little. Floyd, this is No. 62. He's going to be blocking for you today." I looked at the guy in disbelief. "Does he even know the plays?" I found out the answer quickly. On the first play he pulled one way, and our left guard the other. Wham! They smacked right into each other. I thought: "Yeah, this happens all the time on the Packers."

YOU'RE KILLING ME!

If there's one phrase that sticks out in my mind from my days with Lou it was his exasperated phrase, "You're killing me!" Lou said it all the time, probably because we lost so much. That phrase chimed in my head like a grandfather clock stuck on midnight.

The first time he said it to me was in practice. "You're killing me, rookie. You're killing me!" I still heard it after I became one of the top backs in the league. By then, he changed it up a bit: "Floyd, come here. Son, you're killing me."

Despite his claim, Lou must have been reincarnated often because he seemed to have numerous coaching lives. After Denver let him go in 1971, he went back to the Bills, then coached college and high school teams until he was well into his 80s. No matter how tortured and aggravated he seemed, Lou loved coaching. It was his life.

I saw a story about him a few years ago on ESPN. He was coaching a high school team and was telling those kids the same thing: "You're killing me!" he screamed at them. Now approaching 85, nothing's changed. I spoke to Lou recently and he was still going strong.

HIT LIKE A GRANDMOTHER

There's no debating this: Lou had one of the toughest grandmothers in history. I've never met her, but evidently she was better than anyone on our team. Lou told us. Often.

"My grandmother is better than you," he'd yell. "My grandmother hits harder than you."

The guy who probably heard it the most was Chip Myrtle, a linebacker who played for us for six seasons. Chip was a good player. But whenever the defense gave up a big play, Lou would seek Chip out and make him the scapegoat. "Chip, my grandmother is tougher than you," he'd scream.

One time Chip stretched in vain for a tackle and landed in mud. When he got up he had a big chunk wedged between his helmet and facemask. The clod stuck out like a mutant boil. Lou, of course, ignored the effort and got after him again with the grandmother comment. "Geez, Chip. My grandmother—" But Chip ignored him. He refused to turn around. Even during a timeout he wouldn't acknowledge Lou's rants. Finally Lou screamed. "Hey, Chip. At least get that goddamn dirt off your helmet. You look ridiculous!"

Poor Chip. The thing is he had heard it all before coming to the Broncos. Chip played for Lou at Maryland before Saban signed him as a free agent in 1967. Talk about walking a mile to get your feelings hurt. Chip traveled 2,000 miles from the east coast to Denver just to hear Lou taunt him even more as a pro.

NINE STRAIGHT . . . LOSSES

We were all feeling pretty good after our 26-21 victory against the Pats in Week 1 of the '67 season. I was upbeat about the season and happily looked forward to facing the Raiders again in Week 2. This time, however, it was in Oakland and we didn't have Cookie. He was injured in our game against Boston and didn't carry the ball the rest of the season.

To say we lost to the Raiders was to say that Custer lost at Little Big Horn. We were crushed and embarrassed, 51-0. Nothing worked for us, and every time I looked up, the Raiders were scoring. After that ass-whipping, I think we were so stunned we went on to lose another eight games in a row. I had never experienced anything like it.

There were a lot of reasons we lost. Our offense was young, and Lou kept changing the lineup every week in hopes of finding the right mix. We had no cohesion and I had nowhere to run. I was bloody and bruised so much that I felt like I had been in a bad car accident after each game. And Lou just got madder and madder at everyone. During film sessions, no one wanted to sit in the front row because they knew Lou would scream at them. The projector would be humming along and Lou would yell names in the dark. He'd ask a player to speak up, but few of us did. Some guys tried throwing their voices and Lou would start hollering at a spot in the room where no one was sitting. He looked like a man who had gone crazy. But deep inside we knew it was no laughing matter. We needed a win bad.

ORANGE CRUSH

In the midst of our nine-game losing streak that first year, we played the Oilers at old Rice Stadium. This was before the Astrodome was built. Lou was fed up with everyone in that game—especially the kicking team. He had become unglued because the punt and kick coverage teams each allowed long returns that set up easy field goals.

By half-time Lou was his usual boiling-pot self. As we entered the locker room, Lou kicked over our halftime snack, a table of oranges. The fruit bounced all over the place, under benches, into the shower. "No oranges for you!" he snapped. He asked for all the kickoff and punt coverage players to raise their hands. Slowly, each one did. "Go stand over in that corner," he declared. "Now get dressed. You're all fired."

The special-team guys didn't believe him. When halftime was over they tried to get back onto the field, but Lou wouldn't let them. We were stunned. He made them sit and stew in the locker room the rest of the game. We lost, pathetically, 10-6. When we returned to the locker room we found oranges splattered all over the place. The special team players apparently had vented some frustration by decimating the oranges.

GO TAKE A COLD SHOWER

One of the cities we hated playing in was Buffalo. It wasn't so much the weather, although it was usually horrible. It was the "amenities." The Bills played in the aptly named War Memorial Stadium. Heck, its nickname was "The Rockpile." It was a haunting mass of rusting steel. The visiting locker room looked like a dungeon, and the ceiling was always dripping something other than water. If you want an idea of what the stadium was like, watch *The Natural*. The movie was filmed at War Memorial Stadium, and I'm sure they cleaned it up a bit for Robert Redford.

We were 0-9 in our last nine games when we flew to Buffalo to face the Bills in Week 11. It was a predictably rainy day with more wet stuff in the forecast. We were determined to get a win that day for Lou, especially since, as the former Bills coach, he hated losing to them. He repeated before the game, "Don't embarrass me today."

The game turned out to be a muddy mess. I scored from about the 10-yard line in the first quarter, and we built a 21-7 lead. Then the weather got really nasty and the rain turned into a deluge. By the fourth quarter a few of our starters were injured, so Lou started enlisting people to go in on the kickoff team. The downpour was so heavy that no one wanted to go in. Instead we all huddled on the benches with our ponchos hanging over our heads so he couldn't tell who we were. Lou was screaming, "Hey, you. Show me your face. What's your name? Go in on the kickoff team." But some just slumped lower inside their ponchos. Lou even started wrestling with one guy, trying to unveil his identity. I didn't want him doing that to me, so I jumped up and ran onto the field like a wet rat.

Luckily, we held on to win, 21-20. When the gun sounded we didn't even shake hands. We pushed each other out of the way in a mad dash for the locker room. We wanted to get out of the rain, but more importantly we wanted to be first in line for the pitiful showers in the visiting locker room. The hot water only lasted for a few seconds before it turned into the sort of frozen mist that sprays off Niagra Falls in January. Each of us wanted to be the first to enjoy those precious seconds of hot water.

As it turned out, most of us missed the warm water and skipped our shower completely. We flew home covered with mud, but happy to have our second win of the year.

BLOCKING THE BIG CAT

One of our linemen during those early years was tackle Tom Cichowski, a good player, and one of the many guys Lou had coached at Maryland. Tom had good size and could match up pretty well with most anyone. Well, sort of. During a game against the Kansas City Chiefs, Tom was having a tough time against behemoth defensive end Ernie Ladd. At 6-foot-9 and 300 pounds, Ernie was the biggest player I'd ever seen. He was an All-Star earlier with the Chargers, and was finishing his career with the Chiefs. Of course, his nickname was "the Big Cat."

Our line coach, Whitey Dovell, had a pretty simple blocking scheme back then. He'd either call his linemen to block "down," "out," or "fan-it," which meant big man on big man, little man on little man. So if the defensive end was across from the tackle, he would get the end, and I would be responsible for blocking the outside linebacker, the "little" man, which against the Chiefs was future Hall of Famer Bobby Bell. Frankly, I didn't want to block either of those guys. Bobby was a great player, and Ernie, well, was as big as a Ford Explorer.

Ernie was overpowering Tom play after play. It got so bad that by the third quarter he begged me to block Ernie for one play. I said, "Are you crazy? He's 6-foot-9, I'm 5-foot-10. Do the math." I kept refusing him. Finally, on one play I was lined up in the backfield a few yards behind Tom and I heard him say, "Down, down," meaning he was going to block the tackle and leave me to block Ernie.

"Son of a bitch," I murmured under my breath. As the ball snapped I saw Ernie barreling straight at me. I was the only thing between him and the quarterback. I ran and hit him as hard as I could. I aimed for his stomach, but due to the size differential I hit him much lower—in the nuts. I could hear him cursing me like a warden. He was mad as hell. He pushed me back like a folding chair, but I was able to slow him down long enough for our quarterback to get the pass off.

He got up and I apologized profusely. "Sorry, I didn't mean it," I said. "Goddamn it, kid," he yelled and stumbled back to the huddle holding his package. Meanwhile my helmet was sideways. I was looking out my ear hole and had mud all over my face. My neck felt like I got slugged by a two-by-four. "T-t-thanks, Floyd," Tom's voice quivered, "I just needed a break."

WHO WANTS A PIECE OF ME?

We played a few of our six preseason games at neutral sites. Now erase your mind of the glamour spots and foreign locales that teams travel to today, like Tokyo, Japan, or Mexico City, Mexico. We played in Nebraska my rookie year, and a following season we upgraded to Utah. We flew to

Salt Lake City to play a night game against the Patriots. It was at Utes Stadium and the humidity was so bad that a guy could sweat while sitting in a swimming pool.

The Patriots were the designated home team, but we didn't find that out until we were warming up in our home uniforms. Our equipment manager had made a mistake, but Lou said, "No big deal. We'll both wear home jerseys." The officials refused. They said our jerseys were too similar to Boston's red ones. I guess they were right. But jeez, it was a preseason game and the stadium was practically empty.

So we borrowed the Utes' white jerseys. Of course, they were too tight, so we looked like a semi-pro team out there wearing these shrunken jerseys. We played like a semi-pro team, too. By halftime, we were losing 8-3.

Lou wasn't cutting us any slack because of the crappy uniforms, either. "You guys are the worst team I've ever coached," he cried. "You're all a bunch of gutless thieves. You're stealing money. But it's not your fault; it's my fault. I thought you could play this game. But I was wrong. Don't worry—when we get back I'll get some people to replace you, and you won't have to feel bad about yourselves anymore."

Then the heat must have gotten to him because Lou challenged a few guys to fight him. "I can kick anyone's ass on this team and I'm 104. C'mon, who wants a piece of me? Let's go." Right then, defensive end Rex Mirich, who was 6-foot-5, got up and walked toward him. By comparison, Mirich seemed like Bigfoot. Lou wheeled around and knocked over a table of juice. "Let's go, Rex. You think you can take me? Well, I'm not afraid of you," Coach said, both fists shaking noticeably. "Relax, Coach," Rex replied, "I'm just getting some water."

Everyone broke into laughter, and Lou even appeared to lighten up. We went out and won that meaningless game, 16-14.

BULIMIC BOB?

One of the more interesting guys I ever played with was guard Bob Young. He was a short guy (6-foot-1, and 270 pounds) from Texas, but one of the strongest guys I've ever known. Bob joined Denver as a rookie in 1966 and played with us for five years before going on to the St. Louis

Cardinals where he was part of that great offensive line in the 1970s with Dan Dierdorf and Conrad Dobler.

Bob was a big eater, scarfing down food all the time. He didn't seem to care what he ate. Our pregame meal was usually steak and potatoes. But sometimes we had shrimp, which was a big mistake, because Bob *loved* shrimp. Anytime we saw shrimp on the pre-game spread we knew Bob was going to have a long day.

One game Bob had loaded up on so much shrimp he was puking after nearly every play. His face was as green as a well-kept lawn, and he kept throwing up in the huddle. We had to move the huddle a few yards to the left or right after each upchuck. Toward the end of the game it started looking like a well-choreographed dance move. Bob would get sick, and we'd move the huddle in unison, "Step 1-2-3" to the right or "1-2-3" to the left.

Bob also had this high-pitched voice, which was peculiar for such a large man. That whole game he'd say, "Sorry, guys," after each barf, sounding like Kermit the Frog.

A VALUABLE LESSON

The first time we played the Jets at Shea Stadium, one of our tackles, Sam Brunelli, was having a tough time against Verlon Biggs. Biggs was an All-Star and he was beating the crap out of young Sam. Unlike Tom Cichowski, who had left me out on an island blocking Ernie Ladd, Sam asked me to help him double-team Biggs.

In the huddle Sam said, "Floyd, this bastard is beating me to the inside. If you can slow him down inside, then I can keep him from rolling outside." When the ball snapped, Biggs barreled his way to the inside as Sam predicted. Just as he planted his foot, I hit him low to the inside. "Motherf—-er," Biggs howled, "my knee!" He rolled on the ground before teammates helped him. "I'm going to get you, rookie," he roared, as he limped to the sidelines. I apologized several times. The last thing I wanted to be known as was a dirty player, especially as a rookie.

Later Biggs was back on the field. We had built a 26-0 lead, and he was staring at me like I was the last pork chop at the family picnic. I got the ball on a sweep and Biggs was bearing down. As I neared the sideline

Playing the New York Jets brought out the best in us. From 1967-69, our last-place team was 3-1 against Joe Namath's squad. In this 1969 season opener at Mile High, we beat the World Champions 21-19 as I rushed for 104 yards and a touchdown. *Courtesy of the Denver Broncos*

and planted to cut up field, Biggs launched himself at me, spearing me in the shoulder. I fell sideways to the ground; I knew my shoulder was separated immediately. Biggs stood over me and snarled, "That's payback, motherf—-er."

We won 34-24 at Shea, the same place I had scored that long punt return against Pitt while I was in college. This time I returned a punt 72 yards for a touchdown. But the biggest impression made to me that day was the clear message sent by Biggs: the NFL is full of paybacks. The worst thing you could do is hurt a guy, because he'll do all he can to even the score.

THE SILVER LINING

My first couple of years with the Broncos were incredibly frustrating. We had a young team with an assortment of players. Defensively we had a good line, but we couldn't stop the pass. Offensively, though, we weren't very good. We couldn't pass or run. As the No. 1 pick, I thought I could carry the team. But teams crowded the line, and the holes just weren't there for me to run through. Val Pinchbeck, the Broncos public relations director, told me that some of my best runs were just getting back to the line of scrimmage.

That left one area where I could really help the club: the kicking game. My experience returning punts and kickoffs in college allowed me to excel right away in the pros. As a rookie in '67, I led the NFL in punt returns with a 16.9 average, which is still a Broncos record. I also led the league in combined yards two years in a row from 1967-68, and was the only player to return a punt for a touchdown both years.

Still, there was little solace because we weren't winning. I felt the fans deserved better.

CAPTAINS KAMINSKI AND CICHOWSKI?

Rookies are usually never chosen to be team captain. But with 26 rookies on our team and a lot of inexperienced guys from other clubs, Lou made the voting open to everyone. As a 25-year-old rookie, I guess I was more mature than others. For whatever reason, I was chosen the Broncos captain as a rookie, and that continued all nine seasons I played with the Broncos.

Maybe one of the reasons I was voted captain had to do with the shortness of my name. We had a lot of guys with long names. I think it was much easier to jot down "Little" than to try spelling "Kaminski" or "Cichowski."

YOU'RE FIRED!

There was nothing Lou Saban enjoyed more than beating his old team, the Buffalo Bills.

After sneaking out a victory in soggy Buffalo during my rookie year, we were happy to play them at home the following year. Our quarterback that day was rookie Marlin Briscoe, the NFL's first black quarterback. Marlin was small at 5-foot-10 and 175 pounds, but he could roll out, run, and throw with velocity. His efforts earned him the nickname "Marlin the Magician." We drafted him in the 14th round that season from the tiny University of Nebraska-Omaha. He played quarterback in college, but we first tried him at defensive back and flanker.

Steve Tensi was injured again, this time after heaving a ball to some kid 80 yards away during a practice. Lou couldn't believe it. So he continued playing musical quarterbacks. John McCormick, a veteran guy from Massachusetts, played some. Jim LeClair started a couple games. He even tried our rookie punter Joe DiVito at quarterback.

Midway through the season Lou decided to give Marlin a shot. Almost instantly, our entire team seemed to step it up a notch with Marlin in charge. Teams could no longer focus solely on me. They had to account for Marlin's scrambling, which allowed receivers like Eric Crabtree, Al Denson, and tight end Tom Beer more time to get open.

Against Buffalo, Marlin threw two touchdown passes early on to stake us to a 14-0 lead. The Bills came back to make it 14-7. Then right before halftime, Marlin called a screen pass. I caught the ball, broke a tackle, gave a head fake, and outraced everyone down the sidelines for a 66-yard touchdown and a 21-7 halftime lead.

By the fourth quarter it was 28-14, and we were feeling pretty good about things. I was having a good game with 70 yards rushing and over 100 receiving. But our optimism evaporated in a matter of seconds. Ahead 31-22 with two minutes left, we were set to punt when a Bills player broke through to block Joe DiVito's kick, and then run it back to the 3-yard line. The Bills scored again, and suddenly it was 31-29 with a 1:30 left.

Lou was livid. We recovered the onsides kick and Coach grabbed me by the shoulder pads and snarled, "Protect the ball and don't go out of bounds." I thought, "No sweat." I had done this many times at Syracuse. Of course, today the rules allow you to kneel four times; but back then we had to run plays.

I took the handoff and started running left. I don't know what happened, but I tripped on a clump of sod and began losing my balance. To keep from going out of bounds I began waving my arms and the ball just fell out. It seemed like it happened in slow motion. No one even hit me. The ball trickled out of my hands and I lunged for it as I hit the ground. The Bills' George Saimes picked it up and headed for the goal line. I managed to drag him down at the 10. The Bills wasted no time and kicked a field goal to take the lead, 32-31, with just 30 seconds left.

Buffalo was beyond ecstatic. They probably would have made snow angels on the field if there was any snow. And Lou, well, he was angrier than I had ever seen him, his face volcanic red. I went back to receive the kickoff, but he stormed out on the field and shouted, "Get the hell out of here. You're fired." I was shocked. He continued, "I'm serious. You're fired. Highway 25 runs north and south, 70 east and west. Take your pick out of town." My response was simple: "Screw you," I retorted, and began walking off the field toward the locker room.

Everything had turned so quickly. I was furious at myself for fumbling, but even angrier at Lou for embarrassing me in front of my teammates. I thought, "I'm done. I don't need this shit. I've given everything I have to this team." Then halfway up the tunnel, I changed my mind. "There is no way I'm going to be run out of town this way," I muttered. "Not by that fat bastard."

So I turned around and ran back onto the field. By now Fran Lynch, my roommate and backup, had replaced me in the lineup. I went into the huddle and yelled at Fran to get out. He said, "Coach told me to go in for you." I said, "I don't give a shit. I'm not leaving. Someone better get out or we'll get called for 12 men in the huddle."

Saban saw me in the huddle and began shouting from the sideline, "I fired you, Little. Get the hell out, you son of a bitch." I fired back, "F— k you, I'm staying in." Now all the guys were getting upset—especially Fran, who didn't know what to do. The referee came over and demanded that one of us leave the field. I refused to budge, so finally Fran threw up his arms and ran off the field. Lou started screaming at Fran for disobeying him, and the guys in the huddle started yelling at me for pushing Fran out.

I pleaded with Marlin. "You have to do this for me. I don't care how far you throw the ball. I'm headed for the flag. Just throw it as far as you can, and I'll get it."

Down to only 25 seconds and standing on our own 31-yard line, we were out of options. So Marlin looked at me and the rest of the team and said, "Okay, let's give it a shot."

Marlin took the snap and rolled out. I was split right and ran a fly pattern. I noticed right away that there were two guys on me—George Saimes, an All-Star safety, and Booker Edgerson. Marlin waited until the last second before uncorking an arching beauty. It sailed about 65 yards in the air. Sandwiched between these two guys, I knew I'd have to leap high to grab it. I waited till the ball was above my head and jumped as I high as I could. I plucked the precious pigskin out of the air and felt the defenders grabbing at the ball and pulling my facemask the whole way down. When I landed, Edgerson had fallen to the ground and I tried to maneuver away from Saimes only to be gang tackled by him and linebacker Harry Jacobs.

The play had gone for 59 yards. But an official threw a facemask penalty, and suddenly we were in field-goal range with just a few seconds left. Our kicker, Bobby Howfield, who was from Bushey, England, came trotting out to kick the game winner. I grabbed him and said, "Please, please kick this for me." He smiled and said, "Don't worry about it, mate, I got this one," and kicked it straight through the uprights.

The entire crowd went crazy. I guess it was the first big comeback at the miracle mansion later called Mile High Stadium. My teammates were congratulating me, but I barely acknowledged them. I sat there on the bench bawling, knowing this was my last game. Then out of the corner of my eye I saw Lou pointing at me to come over. I said, "F-U!" and walked toward the tunnel. He stared at me with those blistering eyes and ordered me to come over. So I walked over. "What the hell do you want?" I asked. He looked at me and pointed his index finger a few inches from my face. "I'm giving you one more week," he smiled.

Later I found out I had racked up 295 combined yards in that game, a record that stood for more than 25 years. I also heard that before the kick, Lou grabbed Howfield and said, "See that little space next to the door of the dressing room. You can squeeze through it to get to Colfax

The famous "Firing" game against Buffalo in '68 was one of the most exciting games ever played at new Mile High Stadium. I fumbled late in the game and Lou Saban fired me on the spot. I refused to leave the field and redeemed myself with a 59-yard catch that set up the winning field goal by Bobby Howfield. The emotional rollercoaster left me inconsolable after the game. *Courtesy of the Denver Broncos*

Avenue. If you miss this kick, use that exit to get out of here. Don't bother going to the dressing room!"

Now there's a vote of confidence.

A PAIR OF HOMICIDAL MANIACS

I always had a lot of respect for Lou as coach. He didn't always act rationally but, in the heat of battle, real competitors never do. Lou and I were similar in a lot of ways, but it took Lou's annual "psychological" test for both of us to realize it.

The purpose of Lou's test was to determine your personality and what position you were best suited to play in the professional ranks. I was a little nervous about taking the test. Unlike the SATs, there was no way to prepare or study for this. I was afraid he'd think I wasn't smart enough or patient enough to make it in the pros.

I tossed and turned the night before I was to take it. The next morning I went in and took the test. The whole time I kept thinking, "I can't screw this up." Of course, my competitive juices started flowing and my mindset changed. "Screw him. I'll take this test honestly," I decided. "He'll find out what kind of wild man he drafted." I went about answering each question candidly.

A few days later, I got a call from one of his assistants. "Coach Saban wants to see you," the assistant told me.

"About what?" I asked.

"Come to his office, please," the assistant said before hanging up.

My mouth grew dry. "This is it," I thought.

When I showed up, Lou promptly invited me in to his office and shut the door. I sat there nervously for a few minutes while he just stared at me from across the table as if we were in a poker game with all the chips in.

"Floyd, I got your test results back and," he paused, "I've got to say I'm a little shocked." I could feel my palms begin to ooze sweat. "Son, it says here you're a Homicidal Maniac."

My eyes bugged out. I couldn't think of a response so I tried to look puzzled. "Is that, um, bad?" I asked.

Suddenly his cold gaze disappeared, as if he just solved the energy crisis. "No, son, that's great! You're like me. I'm a homicidal maniac, too!" I thought he was joking. But he was serious. "No wonder we've been at each other's throats," he continued. "We're crazy. We're competitive S.O.Bs who'd rather be strapped to the front of a torpedo than lose a game."

According to his test results, my personality was more suited to play linebacker. "They're daredevils," Lou said. "They love contact and crave competition. I was a linebacker and fullback when I played."

So I asked him, "What's a running back's personality supposed to be like?" He laughed. "They're either very smart or a little crazy. Guess what you are?"

As strange as the conversation was, I felt a real connection with Lou, maybe for the first time. He told me that quarterbacks' personalities were similar to generals. "That's why they don't have any friends," he cracked. "Offensive linemen are the smartest. They're very neat and meticulous. Defensive linemen are just like animals. Now you know why we don't even bother to give them playbooks. We just tell them to attack."

From that point on, I wasn't going to worry about hiding who I was. If guys didn't want to win, they were going to incur my "manic" wrath.

SABAN COMPARISONS

I've been asked a few times, which of the current NFL coaches most resembles Lou? That's tough to answer without playing for each coach. But I'd say the coach who mirrors his expressions and demeanor would have to be Bill Cowher of the Steelers. Bill is animated with that well-chiseled jaw and demanding presence, but you can tell his players love him. That was Lou. He screamed, cussed you out, and kicked over his share of tables, but we loved playing for him. Winning made him so happy that it transformed him into another person. After a win, Lou would have this huge shit-eating grin on his face, and he'd grab you by the neck and hug you. His whole life was coaching. He loved every minute of it.

THE HALF-LOAF GAME

The end for Lou Saban as the Broncos coach came weeks before he would eventually resign. The fans had grown impatient by 1971; it was his fifth season as coach, and we still hadn't won more than five games in any season.

During the first game of the '71 season we were playing at home against the Dolphins. Miami, an expansion team just a few years earlier in 1966, was already putting together a team for the ages. They would appear in the next three Super Bowls and go undefeated in '72.

We were on the opposite side of the spectrum. With the retirement of Steve Tensi, Lou went out and traded for two "unknown" quarterbacks. He got rid of all our quarterbacks from the previous year and traded for backups Don Horn from the Packers and Steve Ramsey from the Saints. So 1971 was yet another season with a new quarterback.

The only bright spot on offense was our running game. I had led the NFL in rushing during the first half of the '69 season before a knee injury sidelined me for six games. Then I led the AFC in rushing in '70. The line was gaining confidence and we felt like we could run on anyone. Because I was almost 30, Billy Thompson nicknamed me "Folks," as in "Old Folks." The line got excited whenever Folks' number was called in the huddle.

We played the Dolphins tough that day. They were focused on stopping the run, but the line still managed to help me pound out 70 tough yards. Our defense played exceptional and kept us close. With 2:30 left in the fourth quarter we were up 10-3, and Miami was running out of opportunities. Then on their final possession Bob Griese connected with receiver Paul Warfield for 31 yards to tie the game up.

With over two minutes left we were confident that we could still win. We just needed a field goal. But Lou got conservative in his play calling. He gave me the ball on a simple dive play, and I picked up three yards. Then, on second down Don tripped and fell to the grown for a bizarre nine-yard loss. Now it was third-and-16. Lou called another run that netted four yards, and we punted the ball back to them with 1:20 left. Dolphins safety Jake Scott ran the punt back 18 yards before our kicker,

Jim Turner, hit him in the chest and caused a fumble. Bobby Anderson pounced on it, and just like that we were back in business.

We were jumping up and down. Newly named Mile High Stadium was rocking. We had the Dolphins right where we wanted them. The clocked showed 1:14, more than enough time to drive for a winning field goal. But Lou didn't see it that way. He ran me three times trying to run out the clock and secure a tie. But on my third carry I burst down the right sideline for 11 yards and a first down.

Now with the ball near midfield, Lou decided to take a few chances with 27 seconds left in the game. Don tossed a screen to Bobby for 12 yards. We could have kicked a long field goal then, but Lou wanted to get us closer. Unfortunately, on the next pass attempt, we were called for holding and we were pushed back further—out of field-goal range with just 15 seconds remaining. But it was only second down. There was time for a creative hitch-and-pitch play, or a Hail Mary pass. Instead, Lou was content with a tie and called a simple dive play up the middle. I was hit immediately at the line, and the crowd began booing. The last seconds ticked off, and the game ended, 10-10.

The locker room was like a morgue. We played well enough to win and were upset about being denied the chance. Lou explained that a tie would give us confidence for the rest of the season, while a loss could devastate us before the season got underway. I didn't understand why we were only talking about "a tie or losing." Why wasn't winning an option?

When he met with the press, Lou was asked why he went for the tie. "Half a loaf is better than none," he answered. Well, the media had a field day with that quote, and the Broncos fans were angrier than I had ever seen them. We had lost 51-0 before, but nothing affected them like this tie to a great team. Just like that, Lou's nickname became "Half-Loaf Saban."

The next few games fans threw half-loaves of bread at us. I think some bakery must have special ordered them, because they were extremely compact, like little footballs. And some of our fans had pretty good arms on them. I thought we should give a few of them tryouts.

LOU RESIGNS

After four and a half seasons as the Broncos coach, the losses took their toll on Lou. He had made a lot of trades, hired and fired a lot of players, shuffled the starting lineup each week, but nothing seemed to work. Lou wasn't a patient guy, and the team probably suffered because of it. We needed cohesion. We needed to play with the same quarterback and same offensive unit on a consistent basis.

The Broncos' owners, Gerald and Alan Phipps, were committed to Lou. But despite the owner's support, Lou and his family were bombarded by the wrath of upset fans. His wife and kids were harassed. There was garbage dumped on their lawn, and their house was continuously egged and toilet papered. Lou's son, Tommy, got in a lot of fights at school. They were booed at restaurants. There was nowhere to hide from the disappointment.

Lou's last game as Broncos coach came in Week 9 of the '71 season after an uninspiring 24-10 loss at home to the Bengals in which Cincinnati compiled nearly 500 yards of offense. Our record was 2-6-1 at that point. For the first time, Lou didn't say much after the game. He left the locker room quieter than usual. Something was up. On Monday when we came in for our film session, we heard that Lou had resigned and had already left town. We were told he went back to Buffalo. It bothered me that he never said good-bye, but I guess he had too much pride.

A MILESTONE AMONG THE MUCK

After Lou resigned, Jerry Smith, our offensive line coach, became interim head coach for the remaining five games of the '71 season. We finished 4-9-1, our worst record in four seasons. Somehow, in spite of losing, a one-dimensional offense, Lou quitting, and the fans' vocal frustration, we achieved some Bronco firsts. Thanks to my teammates, I led the entire NFL in rushing with 1,133 yards and became the first 1,000-yard back in Broncos history. Even with a million distractions and even more reasons to quit, the offense banded together and made a statement to the entire NFL that the Broncos could run on anybody.

Truth be told, winning the rushing crown was memorable, but I would have traded it for a playoff appearance.

5

JOHN RALSTON AND THE RAH-RAH BRONCOS

THE COLLEGE COACH

Comparing John Ralston to Lou Saban is like comparing Democrats to Republicans—the two were completely different. John was a college coach who came to the Broncos after leading Stanford to back-to-back Rose Bowl wins. He also was a professional motivational speaker trained at Dale Carnegie who seemed to be a walking video transcript of *How to Win Friends & Influence People*.

When John Ralston became the Broncos' seventh head coach in 1972, the team was in total disarray. One of the first things he said when addressing the team was, "We're going to win the Super Bowl." He said that every year, and it got old after five years of not making the playoffs.

FOOTBALL IS A GAME

John always delivered unusual pregame speeches. In one of his first games as coach we were playing the Redskins in Washington and he must have thought we were a bunch of college freshman. "Gentleman, football is a game," he said, writing the words on a chalkboard. "Make no mistake, anything that ends in B-A-L-L is a game."

Well, in the middle of Ralston's speech, defensive back John Rowser raised his hand and asked, "Coach, what about eyeball and meatball?" John tried to ignore Rowser and continued talking. But the room exploded with laughter, and the speech was as good as over.

TRYING TO CATCH OUR BREATH

Despite Ralston's "inspiring" speeches, we weren't playing well. We were listless during games and it was easy to point the blame. John's training regimen was to work the hell out of us in practices; he was similar to Dick Vermeil in that sense. He held training camp at Cal Poly Pomona, which stands for California State Polytechnic University in Pomona, California, about 30 miles east of Los Angeles. I don't know why we held camp there, considering the site attracted all the smog from L.A. The air quality felt like you were sitting in a garage with the car running. Considering that it was 110 degrees in August, I'm surprised that someone didn't die from heat stroke every day.

Guys were working their asses off in sweltering two-a-days. And this was back when training camp was close to two months long. It got so bad that after the first week some players decided they were going to revolt. "Folks, he's a college coach, and he doesn't know what the hell he's doing," they told me.

My reaction was incredulous. "Hey, what do you guys know about going to the Super Bowl?" I said. "None of us have ever been. We finished the season with four wins last year and our coach was so disgusted he left. Now we've got this new guy and he's won some Rose Bowls. Maybe he can turn it around. If this is what it takes to get to the Promised Land, I'm willing to do that. If you're not, then you have to decide where you want to go, because I'm going to do whatever it takes to win."

To me John Ralston deserved a chance. As a player I was running out of time. I was 30 years old in 1972. I had won two rushing titles and played in four Pro Bowls, but had nothing team-wise to show for it. I had only a few years left, and I wanted to go out a winner.

John Ralston became head coach of the Broncos in 1972 after great success in college. He was a compassionate coach who loved to give big speeches. Despite never gaining the team's full confidence as an NFL coach, he was a smart personnel guy who built the team with great drafts and key trades. When he resigned in 1976 he owned the Broncos' winningest record. *Courtesy of the Denver Broncos*

We continued to suffer through Ralston's practices, but it quickly started affecting everyone—including me. He had these conditioning drills at the end of practice called "Jingle-Jangles" that consisted of running sprints up and down the field touching different yard markers in progression like they do in basketball, except these sprints covered a 100-yard field. Each day there were guys laid out on the ground, throwing up. Some couldn't even get up to go to the locker rooms once practice was over. We had to hustle, too, or the school cafeteria would close.

I started to come around to the guys' point of view. Ralston's practices weren't going to make us better; they were going to kill us. The next day I went to talk to the team but couldn't find them. I looked all over the school and even drove into town. I finally found them later in a small meeting room near the field. I burst into the meeting room and said, "What's going on here?" They said, "Oh, damn. It's Folks. He's found us!"

They continued, "We didn't want to involve you, Folks, but we've had enough. Either he goes, or we're all leaving." I told them, "You're not going anywhere. I'll talk to John today. I'll straighten it out. Do nothing until you hear from me." They looked at me like I was a warden. So I pushed open the door and freed them, "Now get the hell out of here!"

I have to say my teammates were a little afraid of me. I was a very intense player and they didn't think I was always playing with a full deck. Sometimes that worked to my advantage. Guys scrambled out of the meeting room like it was a police raid.

After the meeting I went over and knocked on John's door. He must have just gotten out of the shower, because when he opened the door he was shirtless with a towel wrapped around his shoulders. He said, "Rrrr, c'mon on in. Can I, rrr, get you a coke or something?" John always spoke from his diaphragm. When he wasn't addressing the team he would utter low, monosyllabic sounds.

I cut right to the chase. "Coach," I began, "I have some concerns. The team is not happy with all the conditioning. You're killing them out there." He said, "Rrr, we have to get in shape. Guys are lazy and not willing to work hard." I said, "That's just a couple guys. Most of the guys you have here are professionals. They know how to prepare for the season.

They know what it takes. Even after practice, they'll stay and work on blocking and techniques. We can't do that if we can barely stand."

He wasn't convinced. So I said, "Do me a favor. If you want to see the guys who aren't willing to work, do away with the sprints at the end of one practice and tell the team, 'Those of you who want to stay and work with your position coaches can stay, and those who don't can head into the locker room. You'll see the true professionals.'"

Ralston agreed. After practice he told us we could either hit the showers or stay and work with our coaches. Just as I anticipated, most of the guys—the ones I knew would make the team better—stayed. A dozen or so guys raced from the practice field like it was the last day of school. I stood next to Ralston and said, "Those are the guys you should be concerned with. Leave *us* alone and let us practice." By the end of training camp, each of the players uninterested in staying after practice had been released.

OPERATOR, I REALLY NEED TO MAKE A CALL!

As a married guy with a baby girl I called home at least once a day during camp. This was years before cell phones became a constant fixture in our lives, so we had to use this crappy pay phone in the dorm that would just disconnect on a whim. One time after a particularly long practice I decided to call home before hitting the showers. Every time I put in money the phone hummed, then disconnected. So I called the operator and was cut off in mid-sentence. I got angry. After a three-hour practice, sweat was pouring off me and I was beyond irate. I called one more time, "Operator, I really need to call home. The number is 303-" and I got cut off again.

I went nuts. I grabbed the pay phone and yanked the goddamn thing off the wall and tossed it to the ground. Wires and cables were hanging out of the wall. I looked around thinking, "Holy Shit!" and quickly scooped up the payphone and threw it in a garbage bin. The next day Ralston was steaming. He announced that the "culprit" who "took" the payphone would be fined $10,000. I didn't utter a word. I mean, that was half my salary.

ROOKIE NIGHT

It wasn't all exhausting sprints and complaining at Ralston's training camp. There was always the annual Rookie Show that first-year guys performed to an audience of veterans near the end of camp. Unbeknownst to me, during one particular year—the same year that I had KO'd the payphone—they had prepared a special skit. It started normal enough—a few guys came out dancing and singing. Then they parted to reveal rookie Glen Bailey. He was wearing my No. 44 jersey, and began making a phone call at a cardboard payphone they had constructed. He mimicked my entire tirade, and ended by ripping apart the payphone and heaving it in the garbage.

The whole team roared in approval while I sat there thinking, "Damn, he just rolled me under the bus." I pretended to look puzzled, but I was a nervous wreck. "Oh, boy, this is bad. Real bad." I could feel Ralston's eyes burning a hole in the back of my head. But incredibly, he never said a word to me. I'm guessing he thought I was his only ally.

RAH-RAH JOHN

There were two sides to John. One was the guy who made us practice to the point of exhaustion while reciting "nuggets" of his Dale Carnegie shtick, such as "Every day and every way, just a little bit better."

The other was "Rah-Rah John." That John wanted to be your friend. He wanted you to like him, and he became the team's favorite—albeit, ugliest—cheerleader. During games, whenever I had broken free and was in the open field ready to score, John would be running along with me waving his clipboard. To some degree, it was great to finally have a coach who was giving you the thumbs up instead of the finger. But it took a while to get accustomed to John's enthusiasm.

You know how coaches sometimes gather the kickoff or kick return teams for last-minute instructions before they head onto the field? John actually huddled them up in the middle of the field. The players hated him coming onto the field with them, and it drove the coaches on other teams crazy. We were playing the Bears once and Abe Gibron, a large and in-charge coach of the Bears, was complaining to the ref, Fred Wyant.

"Fred, what's that f—king coach doing on the field?" Abe yelled. "This ain't college!"

ANOTHER COACH, ANOTHER TEST

Early during his first year as head coach, John gathered the troops and said, "Gentlemen, I want to find out a little more about you beyond your height, weight, and 40-time. We're going to be handing out 'questionnaires' for you to answer as honestly as you can."

I said, "Oh, boy, oh, boy. This sure as hell sounds like a test. Not good." Well, damn if it didn't turn out to be the same "personality" test that Lou had given us. After taking the test, I received a call that Ralston wanted to see me. "He's going to give me high marks for candor, just like Lou did," I thought. "He'll be glad he has such an intense, dedicated captain leading his team!"

I got to his office and John opened the door, looking whiter than a piece of sheet rock. "Rrr, c'mon in Floyd, have a seat," he stammered. I began to shut the door behind me when he stopped me. "Oh, p-please. K-keep the door open," he hesitated, "Fresh air—I like to have fresh air." This from the guy who had us practicing at Cal Poly.

"I, uh, got your test back," he said slowly, "and, well, it says here you're a Homicidal Maniac."

"Yup," I nodded, sipping my Coke, "that sounds about right."

"Well, what does that mean?"

"I guess it means if someone f—ks with me I have no problem committing some heinous crime and still be able to enjoy a nice dinner with friends over a bottle of Chianti."

"Well, rrr, that's not normal. I mean, you're our captain. We can't have a leader with, rrr, homicidal tendencies."

I laughed. "Relax, coach. It's just my persona on the football field. Welcome to the National Football League."

For the next few years Ralston tip-toed around me, making sure not to upset me. Whenever we met in his office he'd quickly sit behind his desk so there was some sort of heavy piece of furniture to act as a barrier between us. Just in case.

GOING POSTAL

Once in a while you get a guy on your team who is truly scary. Dwight Harrison was such a guy. As a 6 foot, 1, 187-pound receiver, he wasn't at all imposing. Lou drafted him in the second round of the 1971 draft, between our first pick, tackle Marv Montgomery, and our third, Lyle Alzado. What Lou liked about Dwight wasn't his size, it was his speed.

During the 1971 season—his rookie year—Dwight and I assumed some added responsibility during the game. Our quarterback, Don Horn, threw an incredible six interceptions in the game. As two of the faster players on the team, we had to run down most of the guys who had picked our pocket. After about the fifth interception, Dwight refused to go back on the field. "I'm not playing receiver any more today if he keeps throwing interceptions. I'm tired of making all these tackles," he pleaded. To which I responded, "You can't quit on the team. You're going back in!" We got into a bit of a shoving match on the sidelines until I finally "convinced" him to take the field.

A year later, Dwight got into a fight with Lyle Alzado right before practice. Lyle had teased Dwight about dropping passes, and he told Lyle to shut up and worry about sacking the quarterback more often. Well, Lyle whipped him pretty good. Dwight started telling everyone he was going to kill that "motherf—-er" and wanted to borrow someone's car so he could retrieve his gun. Of course, no one obliged him and he skipped practice to hitchhike 20 miles home in his flip-flops.

When he returned we were in the film room and he kicked the door open and stood there sporting shorts, sunglasses, a Derby hat, and a 357 Magnum. He looked like a character out of *Pulp Fiction*. "Where's that motherf—-er Alzado?" he screamed. "I'm going to kill him." Everyone hit the floor, except me. Like a fool I said, "Dwight, he's not here, and you're not going to kill anyone today." He pointed the gun at me and said, "Get out of my way, Floyd. I don't like you anyway because of the Packers game." I couldn't believe it. That was over a year ago!

Until that day, I had never had a gun pointed at me. I can tell you it's quite an effective laxative. I backed off, and Coach Ralston was eventually able to coax Dwight into his office. He must have used all his Dale Carnegie powers of persuasion to get him to put his gun away. Dwight was in tears the whole time. He finally handed over his gun, and was promptly traded to Buffalo to be reunited with Lou. In exchange, we got receiver Haven Moses. Lou converted Dwight to defensive back and, incredibly, he played another nine seasons with a couple other teams.

As horrifying as the event was, I'd have to say it was almost worth having a gun pointed at me if it meant we could get Haven Moses on our team.

BETTER GM THAN COACH

Say what you want about John's coaching methods. The guy was a great personnel man. We never seemed to win the big games under his leadership but, boy, did he bring in some great talent. During his tenure John traded for Charley Johnson, Bobby Maples, Haven Moses, Jon Keyworth, and Ray May. And he drafted Riley Odoms, Otis Armstrong, Barney Chavous, Paul Howard, Tom Jackson, Randy Gradishar, Claudie Minor, Louis Wright, Rick Upchurch, Rubin Carter, and Steve Foley. Five of those fellas became Ring of Famers, and a few more deserve to be. Many of these players were the guys Red Miller took to the Super Bowl in '77.

For some reason John has been vilified since his dismissal in '76. The fact is he became the first coach to turn the Broncos into a winner. His record of 34-33-3 is dramatically better than Lou's 20-42-3 record.

THE DIRTY DOZEN

After I retired in 1975 there was no one to act as a buffer between the team and Coach Ralston. Things changed quickly. Charley Johnson retired, meaning John turned to backup Steve Ramsey to lead the team. The players wanted John to go out and get an established quarterback. Steve became the starter and did an admirable job leading Denver to its best record ever at 9-5. But in the biggest game of the season—a showdown with the Patriots at Foxboro in which a win would almost assure the Broncos their first playoff berth—the team got whipped 38-14, and both Ralston and Ramsey received most of the blame.

The matchup was supposed to be a close, tough-as-nails contest. But by halftime we were down 31-0. Ramsey completed only about a third of his passes and had three interceptions. As a result the team decided the coach needed to go at the end of the '76 season. Lyle became the Broncos' "inspirational" leader in John's ouster. More than 75 percent of the team signed a petition asking for Coach's dismissal, a document they casually left for the press to find.

Who was the Dirty Dozen? They were the team's biggest stars. Lyle, Billy Thompson, Tommy Jackson, Mike Current, Paul Smith, Haven Moses, Rick Upchurch, Billy Van Heusen, Tommy Lyons, Louis Wright, Otis Armstrong, and Riley Odoms. The bottom line about Ralston, they claimed, was that he simply was not a good coach and couldn't win the big games. That much became clear against New England, as well as earlier in the season versus Houston when offensive coordinator Max Coley was sick, forcing John to call the plays for the first time. It was evident on that day that he didn't know what he was doing. He even tried to get Charley Johnson, who was retired and sitting in the stands, to come down to the field and help. "Our offense," Billy Thompson said famously, "was like a ballet—one, two, three, kick!"

After five seasons the Broncos had become one of the better teams in the AFC, but the fans and the team desperately wanted more. John's positive spin had run out of yarn.

STAN THE MAN

We had one of the best defensive lines in the league when Lou was the head coach, and everyone knew why: Stan Jones, our line coach. Elected to the Hall of Fame in 1991 after a stellar career with the Bears in the 1950s, Stan was a natural leader who knew how to motivate players because he had been a great one himself. He didn't just have strong players on the defensive line, he had specimens—Rich Jackson, Lyle Alzado, Paul Smith, Rex Mirich, Dave Costa, Pete Duranko, and Jerry Inman.

Stan had these guys living in the weight room, where he somehow made working out fun. His linemen looked like they were on vacation. They adhered to a different code than the rest of us: they went to meetings with their shirttails hanging out; they didn't shave; heck, they didn't even have playbooks. In practice Stan would tell them to "just hit the guy in front of you!" Lou didn't yell at them much because they were Stan's boys. Stan would just sit there puffing on a cigar with his rottweiler (that hated people) at his side, and implore his guys to throw some iron around.

We all wanted to be defensive linemen and play for Stan. Rex Mirich got me into lifting with the linemen. I felt connected with their battle-in-the-trenches mentality. After Lou resigned and Stan left to coach with him in Buffalo, I continued working out with linemen.

SAM RUTIGLIANO

I loved Hunter Enis. He was a former Broncos quarterback and my backfield coach when Lou was here. But the one coach I always wanted to play for was Sam Rutigliano. He was the receivers coach and was a real student of the game. He constantly talked about technique, which as a smaller guy I completely understood. Sam used to say that football was "combat with a little finesse thrown in." I always liked that.

After retiring I became a TV analyst for NBC Sports. I was in Seattle doing a Browns game when Art Modell stopped by the booth and asked me what I thought about Sam as a possible head coach. I told him, "Let's put it this way. I'm retired. I have no desire to play. But if Sam were my coach, not only would I come back. I'd play for free." A couple nights later, I received a phone call at 2 a.m. My first thought was, "Who died?" But it was Sam on the other end, bawling. "I was just offered the Browns coaching position," he said. He thanked me for my endorsement and offered me any coaching job on the team. I graciously declined. Looking back, if I had taken the job I'd probably be a head coach by now.

MAD MAX

Max Coley came by way of the Steelers and joined John Ralston's coaching staff in 1972. As the offensive coordinator and backfield coach, he brought with him Pittsburgh's trap-blocking schemes. We ran traps, fake traps, draws, and more screens than ever. The funny thing was we seemed to have the greatest success against the Steelers. Pittsburgh's defensive ends hated playing us the most. Dwight White and L.C. Greenwood never knew where a block was coming. They might get hit by a guard, a tight end, or a fullback.

Despite having a far worse record than the Steelers, during the five games we played against them in my career, we were 3-1-1 head to head. Two of those wins even happened in Pittsburgh.

6

CAST OF CHARACTERS

PAY ME OR TRADE ME

Of the dozens of quarterbacks who played for the Broncos during my nine-year career, none made a more lasting impact on professional football than Marlin Briscoe. On September 29, 1968, we were playing the Boston Patriots when Marlin came into the game in the fourth quarter to take over at quarterback. That simple substitution was of great significance: It marked the first time an African-American had ever quarterbacked in an NFL game.

Marlin was undersized for his position. Yet his elusive, improvisational style and rocket arm earned him the nickname "Marlin the Magician." In his lone rookie season with the Broncos, he threw for 1,589 yards and a rookie team-record 14 touchdown passes. But if anyone knew how talented Marlin was, it was Marlin. Following his rookie season, Marlin met with coach Lou Saban, who asked him to switch to receiver. Marlin refused. He wanted to stay at quarterback and become the highest paid player on the team.

At the time, I was the Broncos' highest paid player, earning an extraordinary $26,000 a year. Lou tried to reason with Marlin, telling

One of the Broncos' many quarterbacks was Marlin Briscoe (15), the NFL's first African-American quarterback. As a rookie, Marlin took over when starter Steve Tensi got hurt. His strong arm and scrambling ability instantly upgraded our offense. Here he is pitching he ball to me in a 1968 game versus the Raiders.
Courtesy of the Denver Broncos

him, "You can't make more than Floyd. He's our No. 1 pick and he does everything: rushing, receiving, and returning punts, and kickoffs."

Marlin's response? "Well, Floyd's a fool to do all that. I'm not going to play for less than him—pay me or trade me."

Saban did one better. He cut Marlin, who wound up in Buffalo. He never played quarterback again. The Bills converted him to receiver like Lou had wanted to do, and two seasons later he made the Pro Bowl. Later in his career he earned two Super Bowl rings with the Dolphins. Still, I'm convinced Marlin would have enjoyed a successful career at quarterback had he been given the opportunity to play more than that one season behind center.

GOLF ANYONE?

Billy Thompson is one of the all-time great Broncos. "BT" was the first Bronco to play 13 seasons, over which time he only missed a total of three games. Frankly, he was the most versatile defensive back who ever played. A Pro Bowler, he excelled at both corner and safety and, as a rookie in 1969, he became the only player in NFL history to lead the league in both kickoff and punt returns. And he also had 40 career interceptions. Before Billy joined the Broncos, our secondary was pretty suspect. Lou went out and drafted six defensive backs in 1969, but Billy was the only one who stuck. Later we traded for Leroy Mitchell, who added more stability.

Billy's a Ring of Fame member and now the Broncos Director of Alumni Relations. He's also a heck of a golfer who consistently shoots in the low 70s. But when he first joined the Broncos, Billy had never picked up a golf club. I had learned to play golf at Syracuse. So one day I took Billy and Nemiah Wilson to City Park to show them how to play. That first time we must have lost 12 dozen balls. The squirrels were afraid for their lives. On one shot Billy hit the ball into some trees and it somehow bounced out and onto the fairway. "You must have used your Tree-wood," I cracked.

But Billy continued to improve over the years. On one rainy Christmas day we were out on the course playing for $1 a hole. The day started with drizzle, and by the time we were on the back nine the rain was really coming down. Of course, since there was "big" money involved, we kept playing. We were having a good time until Billy decided to use a wedge on this flooded green to putt his ball.

I told him, "You're not allowed to use a wedge. You'll leave a divot on the ground."

"I can putt with any club I want," he replied. "I'm using my wedge."

"No, you can't," I demanded.

Back and forth we argued for 20 minutes, standing soaking wet in this deluge like a pair of hard-headed idiots. Nemiah thought we were nuts and left. I guess that's what happens when ultra-competitive Broncos face off against one another on the golf course.

WE DON'T NEED NO STINKIN' RODS

On days off when we weren't arguing on the golf course, Billy and I would head up to the mountains near a lake where I had a place with a boat and a few snowmobiles. One time after a particularly brutal game we decided to head up there and do some fishing. We must have been out on the lake for hours without a single bite.

After a few beers we got creative and thought of a "better way" to catch fish. We tossed our fishing rods aside and dumped a bottle of salmon eggs—which to fish are as exquisite as caviar is to people—in the water. In just a few minutes all these bass had surrounded the boat. Without letting go of our precious beer, we began grabbing at the fish with our free hands. (I guess it didn't occur to us to put the beers down.)

We spent the next hour flailing desperately at these fish, spilling beer and splashing water everywhere. Imagine two 200-pound guys jumping from side to side on a little motorboat swaying back and forth on a lake. By the end of the day we were tired and wet—and we had no fish to show for it. So we decided to scare the shit out of the fish by doing cannon balls off the side of the boat. Yup, the picture of maturity.

LABORATORY RATS

I can't recall a time when there wasn't a Broncos receiver wearing jersey No. 80. Today, of course, it belongs to Rod Smith, a phenomenal player and a future Ring-of-Famer. Before him Mark Jackson—one of the "Three Amigos"—wore it. And before Mark, it belonged to Rick Upchurch, one of the most exciting Bronco players ever.

The guy who wore 80 before Rick was a pretty good receiver in his own right. At 6-foot-1, and 210 pounds, Jerry Simmons was a gifted, fluid receiver who played for the Broncos from 1970-74. He was our only receiving threat those first couple years when we were playing musical quarterbacks. When quarterback Charley Johnson came on board in '72, we traded for receiver Haven Moses from Buffalo. Jerry and Haven gave us bookend receivers who could catch any pass, short or deep.

Jerry was quite the unique jokester. He loved to instigate things, considering his teammates to be amusing science experiments as if he

Ring of Famer Billy Thompson—"BT"—was a gifted player. During his 13-year career he excelled at cornerback, safety, and returning punts and kickoffs. He's also a heck of a golfer, although his etiquette is questionable! *Courtesy of the Denver Broncos*

were Dr. Evil. He liked to get two guys mad at each other, then sit back and watch them go at it like he was at a movie premiere. All he needed was a bag of popcorn.

He'd say things like, "Hey, Floyd. Haven says he can beat you in the 40 wearing loafers." And then he'd turn around to Haven and say, "Floyd thinks you're one of the slowest receivers in the league. Lyle Alzado is faster than you." The next thing you know, Haven and I would be challenging each other to a race—in the locker room.

THE BEST QB

Of all the quarterbacks I played with, Charley Johnson was the best. He's a real-life genius with a Ph.D. in Chemical Engineering. Today, he's the head of the Chemical Engineering Department at New Mexico State, his alma mater.

On the field, Charley was a true field general who never received the national recognition that he deserved. He was one of the better quarterbacks in the league for two decades, playing nine years with the Cardinals and two with the Oilers in addition to his four years in Denver. Bronco fans remember his achievements and the organization certainly honored his contributions by electing him to the Ring of Fame in 1986. But when great quarterbacks of his era are mentioned by the media, his name is never on the list. When he retired in 1975, Charley ranked 13th all-time in passing yards, and 15th in touchdown passes. He threw for 445 yards and six touchdowns in a game, led the NFL in passing yards in 1964, and appeared on the cover of *Sports Illustrated* twice while with the Cardinals.

When John Ralston decided to bring in a veteran quarterback to lead the Broncos in 1972, he didn't hesitate to send a third-round pick to Houston for Charley's services. Charley brought instant credibility to the Broncos quarterback position, which was considered a weak link. In my nine seasons with the Broncos, no less than 35 players were given a shot at the quarterback's job.

Charley was a true Texan who didn't mince words. He had learned from the best, honing his craft in the mid-'60s when the Cardinals hired his idol, Bobby Layne, to tutor him. Charley had his own ideas on the

When it comes to great leaders, Charley Johnson (12) was the most overlooked quarterback of my era. He played 15 seasons and was the consummate professional. We finally got stability at quarterback when John Ralston traded for Charley in 1972. That's Jerry Simmons (80) in motion. *Courtesy of the Denver Broncos*

field, too. He didn't simply take orders from the sidelines. If a play would come in from the coach and Charley didn't agree with the call, he would grimace and say, "Forget that, here's what we're going to do." He'd change the play right in the huddle, oftentimes drawing it up from scratch.

"Haven," he would say, "instead of running a down and out, I want you to run a post and clear out the left side. Now, Folks, you're going to run a flair route to that side. The Will backer [weak side linebacker] will be coming hard, so make sure you chip him before you get out, or he'll be catching your pass." Then he'd look me in the eyes. "Folks, it's on you. Better catch that damn pass or the coach is going to chew my ass for changing the play."

Charley took control of a huddle and we all believed in him. But one time I dropped an easy pass over the middle with no defender in sight. Charley didn't even look at me in the following huddle. He simply said, "Same play to the same asshole on two."

Ouch.

BED CHECK

Besides trading for Charley Johnson, Coach Ralston also grabbed his Houston sidekick, center Bobby Maples. The whole makeup of the team changed when they joined Denver, and it's no coincidence that the team began to ascend to the next level at that time. They were two incredible leaders and gave our offense much more punch. As intense and tough as they were on the field, both "Mapes" and Charley were laid-back jokers off it. The two roomed together and were inseparable. If Charley was playing a joke on someone, you can bet Mapes was his accomplice.

During training camp one year Mapes and Charley decided to "play up" their inseparable reputation. One night during bed check, a coach gave the customary one knock and opened their door and found Mapes under Charley's covers in bed. The coach stood there with his jaw to the floor as Bobby stuck his head out of bed and smiled, "Charley, you should have told me someone was coming in!"

After that the coach just bypassed their room.

THE HACK AND THE CRITTERS

Dale Hackbart and Ken Criter were two great special teams players. Dale played only one season for us (in 1973) but is credited for making one of the biggest all-time hits—although it cost him dearly. We were playing the Bengals, and Boobie Clark, Cincinnati's 230-pound monster fullback, was returning a kick. Dale really leveled Boobie and both crumpled to the ground. While Boobie stayed on the ground for some time, "The Hack" got up and walked to the sidelines.

"I think I'm hurt," he said to our trainer.

"Where?" replied the trainer.

"In my neck."

"What does it feel like?" asked the trainer.

"It feels like something snapped," Dale said.

He was quickly taken in for X-rays. Sure enough, "The Hack" had broken his neck.

Ken Criter, on the other hand, was a mainstay special teams ace who played for us from 1969-74. He made some incredible hits and touchdown-saving tackles as a Bronco. In honor of his performance and dedication, our special teams were nicknamed "Criter's Critters."

'YOU, YOU' NEVERMIND 'ME, ME'

There are a number of Broncos who I believe are worthy of the team's Ring of Fame. One player who is way overdue is wide receiver Rick Upchurch. I only got to play with Rick for one season, his rookie year in 1975. But I was blown away by his talent, and he quickly became one of the most dangerous playmakers in the league. During his nine-year career, he returned eight punts for touchdowns and was voted to four Pro Bowls.

Rick showed the NFL that he was something special in his very first game in the 1975 season opener. We were playing the Chiefs at home and Rick hadn't even had time to get his decals placed on his helmet yet. He and I were returning kicks that game. (Yup, at 33 years old, I was still back there "being a fool," as Marlin Briscoe put it.)

While awaiting the first kickoff, I revealed to Rick my "scientific" approach to returning kicks. "Rick, if the ball is coming toward you, I'll say, 'You, you,' meaning you return it. If it looks like it's coming to me, I'll say 'Me, me,' and I'll take it."

This seemed simple enough, right? Well, the first kickoff sailed through the air, and the ball was clearly headed toward Rick, so I yelled "You, you." He caught the ball and returned it 25 yards. Later in the game on the second kickoff, I noticed the ball was kicked pretty far. I yelled at him, "You, you. No, no! Down it in the end zone." Rick got confused and ran back five yards deep into the end zone, caught the ball and returned it 25 yards. Being the intense veteran I was, I scolded him, "Never return a kick that deep. Just down it!" He looked at me with those glassy rookie eyes and apologized.

Late in the game, Kansas City kicked off, and the ball was heading toward Rick once again. I screamed, "You, You." Then it started sailing deeper. "No, no," I shouted. Then, the wind shifted and the ball came straight back over my head. "Oh, shit!" I cried. Against my own rules, I fielded the ball deep in the end zone, and instead of downing it I returned it 25 yards. Rick just glared at me. I had a shit-eating grin as I jogged off the field.

Rick had an incredible NFL debut that game, piling up 284 combined yards, including a record 90-yard touchdown catch from Charley Johnson. We won in a 37-33 thriller, but by the end of the day I could tell he didn't want to return kicks with me anymore. I totally confused the kid.

THE DREADED PHONE CALL

Fran Lynch not only was my dependable backup for all nine seasons, he was my roommate at summer camp and on the road. He was a tough kid from Connecticut, like me, who was drafted the same year in the fifth round. Fran was considered a long shot to stick in the NFL, but he developed into the epitome of a team player: hardworking, disciplined, unselfish, and a true professional. To give you an idea of his dedication and resiliency, he became the first player to suit up for the Broncos for 10 seasons.

What motivated him to be so successful and achieve such longevity was probably his biggest fear—being cut. Each camp he would torture himself with negative thoughts, thinking that this was the year he'd finally be sent home. Fran would hole himself up in his room and become a nervous wreck near the end of each camp. Every time the phone rang, he was afraid to answer it.

On one occasion, Charley Johnson and I decided to play a joke on Fran. The phone rang at 7 a.m. one morning during camp. I answered the phone. "Hello? Oh, hi coach," I said. "Fran? Yes, he's here. … What? You want him to come to your office and bring his playbook? Okay, I'll tell him." Meanwhile, Charley was on the other end of the line, laughing hysterically. I got off the phone and turned to Fran, who had turned 10 shades whiter than a loaf of Wonder Bread.

"Coach wants to see you," I told him.

"Shit, this is it!" he shook.

"Don't worry, Fran. I'll go with you. Just don't forget your playbook."

As Fran slowly walked down the steps to the lobby, he looked up and saw Charley and Bobby Maples, those Texas side splitters, clutching their stomachs and stomping the ground with their feet. Fran's ghost-white body turned the color of Tabasco. "You bastards!" he screamed, throwing his playbook at them.

"C'mon Fran," Bobby crooned, "We're late for breakfast."

NAKED DREAMS

The one thing I noticed early on about Fran was his utter lack of self-consciousness about his body. He used to walk around naked all the time in the room. "Floyd, you're not bothered by this, right?" he'd presume. I'd laugh awkwardly because I didn't know how to respond.

He'd sleep naked, too. Before games he would spread buck-naked on his bed and ask me if it was okay to drink a couple beers, like I was his coach and he needed my permission. It was almost like a ritual.

He'd say, "Do you think it's okay if I have a couple beers?"

I'd say, "Fran, let me ask you, did you play last week?"

"No," he'd answer.

"Did you play the week before?"

"No."

"So, it really doesn't matter how much you drink," I'd conclude.

He'd laugh, crack a few beers open, and pass out naked. Not a good sight. Around that time, Dave Kopay, a former 49ers running back, had shocked the NFL by admitting that he was gay and announcing that there were gay players on every NFL team. With that knowledge in mind, I decided to have a little fun at Fran's expense. Truth be told, I really just wanted him to put his clothes on once in a while.

The night before a game I waited for Fran to drink his beer and get to the brink of passing out—right when his eyes began to close. Then I quietly took off my pants and underwear and snuck around the other side of his bed and nudged my foot on his back. Fran awoke startled and his eyes bugged out.

"W-what are you doing?" he screamed.

"Huh?" I said. "Oh, I thought you were asleep."

"What, the hell!" he blurted. "Are you serious?"

I just got up, nonchalantly put on my clothes, and climbed back into my bed. For the first time Fran hurriedly put on his underwear, pants, and shirt, and pulled his covers up to his chin. He stayed up the whole night staring at me. I had to think of drowning kittens to keep from laughing. But it worked: He never walked around naked again. For the next several years he'd sidle up to me once in a while and whisper, "Were you serious?"

Sometimes you have to use extreme measures to get your point across.

WILD LYLE

When Lyle Alzado joined the Broncos as a fourth-round pick from tiny Yankton College (South Dakota) in 1971, I was given the challenging job of being one of his mentors. I was assigned as his traveling partner. It was my job to sit with him on planes and bus rides and act as a calming influence. For some reason, he listened to me.

While Rich Jackson and Paul Smith took him under their wings to make him a better player, I tried to make him a better professional. Lyle was a tremendous guy to know. He had a huge heart and a natural affinity for children. He became a fixture in Denver and started joining me for charity events.

But away from the public, Lyle was moody and easily irritated. He was a tough, hyper kid from Long Island, New York, and sometimes he was out of control with his emotions, which I could relate to since I also had a short fuse. Some guys were afraid of him and it wasn't uncommon to see him sitting by himself, struggling with his own thoughts. He so much wanted to be a great player; he used to always ask me, "What do I need to do to be a Pro Bowler?" I told him that he needed to establish the mindset that every play is your last play. "Imagine you have an imaginary switch under your arm," I'd tell him, "low, medium, and high. You turn it on high and pretend someone breaks it off, so your only speed is all out."

"The Wild Child." Lyle Alzado was an emotional, talented player who I became a mentor to during his early years with the Broncos. He wanted so much to be famous, and finally was, winning a Super Bowl with the Raiders. Unfortunately, his admitted steroid use cut short his life. *Courtesy of the Denver Broncos*

Lyle began to heed my advice while learning techniques from Rich and Paul. Soon he was turning heads with his play on the field. Unfortunately, early on he developed some narcissistic tendencies. He loved hearing his name on the public address announcement and would sometimes jump offsides on purpose—just so he could hear his name. On a few occasions he even jumped offsides on third-and-5 situations, which pissed off his defensive mates. "C'mon, Lyle, that's another four downs!" they'd yell. Guys would come up to me and say, "Folks, you gotta get him to stop that." I'd pull Lyle aside and tell him, "Lyle, a player's reputation is what defines him. You don't want to be known as a sloppy player. You want to be known as someone who never takes a play off. That's a true professional."

Lyle stopped purposely jumping offsides shortly thereafter and became an extremely dedicated player. After I retired in '75 he became a Pro Bowl end and a leader of the Orange Crush defense that propelled Denver to its first Super Bowl in '77. After a contract dispute he was traded to the Cleveland Browns in '79, and four years later he won a Super Bowl with the Los Angeles Raiders. He finally became the national celebrity he always wanted to be with the Raiders, and sadly because of his steriod use, changed a lot of people's perceptions about professional football.

MUHAMMAD COMES TO THE MOUNTAINS

When asked who his hero was, Lyle never hesitated in answering: "Muhammad Ali." As a youngster Lyle was a Golden Gloves champion. He was born a street fighter, and I think he looked at Ali as the type of fighter he wanted to be—graceful, tough, and a popular showman.

On July 14, 1979, Lyle got his lifelong dream and fought Ali at Mile High Stadium in a charity event. The Broncos had been to the Super Bowl the year before and Ali had retired for the time being. Lyle had asked me to be in his corner for the fight, to serve as a Second, the person who assists the trainer, rinses the mouthpiece, and so on. His other Second for the match was the beautiful actress Susan St. James, who later married NBC Sports president Dick Ebersol.

Lyle trained for weeks for the bout. "It's four rounds," he kept telling me. "I've got to last four rounds. I can't let him knock me out." Lyle was confident until a few hours before the fight when one of the promoters came in and announced the fight had been switched from a four-rounder to a six-round bout. Lyle freaked. "Are they shitting me?" he exploded. "I trained for four rounds, I can't go six." Then he was told to start drinking a lot of liquids because it was 90 degrees outside. "I won't last. I'll die out there," he shook. We spent the next few hours trying to calm him down. But, boy, he was nervous.

Lyle entered the ring to a crowd of 40,000 people cheering him on, and his whole demeanor changed. He not only went all six rounds against the greatest fighter in the world, he dished out some punishment, too. He fought Ali, the temperature, and the altitude with tremendous courage. I have to say I was so proud of Lyle that day.

I probably wasn't the best Second, either. I was in awe of being so close to Ali that sometimes I forgot to bring Lyle water. He kept saying, "Where's the water, Floyd? Where's the f——-ing water!"

THE END

I've been asked on plenty of occasions about Lyle's use of steroids. As someone who never even took painkillers—let alone performance-enhancing drugs—I'm probably not the best person to ask. I never saw any evidence of steroid use when I played with him. Sure, he was moody. But Lyle was that way from the first day I met him. He never changed. Physically, though, I saw quite a change after he joined the Raiders.

Lyle had always been incredibly sweet and nice to my daughters. We were neighbors and my kids would go over to his house on occasion. He had this big dog, a husky named Bronco, whom my daughters loved. One time during the 1980s, the Raiders were playing the Broncos in Los Angeles and I took my daughters to the game. "Can we see Lyle?" my girls pleaded. So we went down on the field and Lyle came over and picked them up just as he had done when they were little. I looked at Lyle and he seemed like a different guy. He was a lot bigger than when I played with him—at least 30 pounds heavier and cut like a washboard.

He finally won a Super Bowl with the Raiders. When he got the brain tumor and blamed it on steroids, I think he was embarrassed of his situation. But he also wanted to let kids know that they shouldn't follow in his footsteps. By being honest and admitting his wrongs, he continued to show how much he cared about kids.

As his illness set in, Lyle refused to see me, telling people he didn't want me to see him deteriorating. He said that Howie Long and I were the two friends he respected the most. I really miss him.

LAUGHING AT HIMSELF

One of the true pros I played with was Pete Duranko. He was a mainstay on our formidable defensive line for eight seasons and was loved by everyone.

During one team meeting, Coach Saban was ranting and raving about how we really needed to get after our upcoming opponent. It had been a rather intense week, and Pete decided it was time for some levity. He placed a laughing box in the back of the room, and every time Lou spoke the gizmo started in with this infectious giggle. Lou kept saying, "Who's laughing? Why, I'm going to fire your ass!" But he quickly realized that no one was laughing; it was a machine. After a couple minutes even Lou couldn't keep himself from laughing.

There are only a few guys who could get Lou to laugh at himself. Pete was one of them. Tragically, he's now suffering from Lou Gehrig's Disease. My heart goes out to him and his family. It was an honor to play with him.

UNSUNG HEROES

Of all the Broncos from my era, the offensive linemen never got the credit they deserved. Think about it: During my career, from 1967-75, only three members of the offensive line—guard George Goeddeke, tackle Mike Current, and center Larry Kaminski—played in an AFL All-Star game. Those appearances came during the '60s. When the leagues merged in 1970, none were ever voted to the Pro Bowl. That's incredible when you consider that I led the AFC in rushing two years straight, won the NFL rushing crown in '71, led the NFL in rushing touchdowns in '73, and during a six-year period from 1968-73 had more yards rushing and more yards from scrimmage than anyone. I mean someone was blocking for me, right?

Without the line's incredible work ethic and dedication, I wouldn't have won a rushing crown, played in five Pro Bowls, and retired as the NFL's seventh all-time rusher. Sure, it took a few seasons to gain some experience and stability on the line. But when they finally jelled in my fourth season, in my mind, they were among the finest in the league.

When Charley was our quarterback he would call plays only after getting input from the line. A play would come in for me to run through the six hole, and Charley would say, "Let's forget about the six; where can we pick up three yards?"

"Run it behind me," Larron Jackson would yell.

"No, I own my guy," Mike Current would chime in. "Run behind me."

Charley would listen and call the play based on their feedback. When I ran the ball my line would get all excited. "Folks is running the ball," they'd smile. "Let's do it for Folks!"

MAPES

Center Bobby Maples may have been our quickest lineman. He was a lot like current center Tom Nalen. He wasn't big, but he was a great technician, an aggressive player who always had a hat on someone. He was a leader and played all out until the whistle blew. If you look at any photos of me running, you'll probably see Bobby on the ground after laying some wood.

In my last game at Mile High, I went off tackle and turned the corner downfield. Bobby got off his first block and ran past me to make another one. On the way back to the huddle he said, "Floyd, when I can make a block and pass you to hit someone else it's time for you to retire." I looked at him, smiled, and said, "You dirty bastard!"

Bobby passed away a few years ago. I think a great epitaph would have been, "He always had a hat on someone."

BIG BUDDHA

Larron "Big Buddha" Jackson joined the Broncos in a trade with Houston in '71. At 6-foot-3, and 270 pounds, he was a huge guard for that era. We decided that about 60 percent of Larron's weight, though, came from his butt. He had the biggest backside of anyone in the league. That's how he got the nickname, "Big Buddha." It just fit.

Some of my best runs came from following his blocks on sweeps. Hiding behind his big ass gave me an extra half-second to make my cut and head up field.

Today he's a minister at a church in Denver. When I see him at alumni events I tease him, "Larron, your butt is so big that if you ever want to haul ass, you'd have to make two trips!"

BRUNO

Sam Brunelli played six years for the Broncos, from 1966-71, and was a tough, strong-as-hell guard and tackle. We nicknamed him "Blowfish" because he had these huge Popeye forearms and used to pretend he was pumping them up by blowing into his thumbs.

Sam also wore three different jersey numbers during his Broncos career—64, 68, and 72. I used to tease him that they were based on his three highest IQ scores. He'd say, "I'm smarter than I look." I'd reply, "I sure hope so!"

THE BRAWL

On every level of my football career there was an "episode" where guys on my team found out exactly how intense I was about football. The biggest confrontation I had as a Bronco was with tackle Mike Current. It was our rookie season and we were playing the Raiders and, as usual, they were handing our asses to us. I was getting the shit beat out of me and at halftime I heard Mike complaining that he couldn't block Oakland's defensive end, Ike Lassiter. Our line coach, Whitey Dovell, was imploring him to get tough. But Mike kept sulking. "I can't," he said. "I just can't block him!"

Unlike today, the Broncos offensive line never got the credit it deserved under Coach Saban or Coach Ralston. I would have never become the NFL's seventh all-time rusher without them. Here I turn the corner in a '73 game behind Larron "Big Buddha" Jackson (68), Marv Montgomery (78), and center Bobby Maples (50), who is on the ground, as usual, after sacrificing his body with another great block.
Courtesy of the Denver Broncos

Well, I couldn't believe this was coming from a pro. I snapped. I jumped up, grabbed Mike, and body slammed him to the ground. He was in shock. The whole team couldn't believe it. Guys were trying to peel me off him, but I wouldn't let go. I told him he didn't deserve to play professional football. "How are you going to beat Lassiter when you can't even beat my ass," I screamed. "You've already quit and there's still a half to play. You might as well get the hell out of here."

Mike was so mad he stared at me in the huddle the rest of game. He didn't utter a word but his whole attitude changed. He dominated Lassiter the rest of the game. As Mike walked off the field afterwards, I said, "Mike, whatever happened at halftime I did it because I felt it needed to be done. If you want to go at it with me after we get out of the locker room, I'll meet you back here and give you that opportunity. No one needs to know but us."

He didn't say anything in response and never met me afterwards. Mike became a great player, but that episode unfortunately kept us from becoming close friends. Then a couple years after I retired, I was covering a Buccaneers game as a TV analyst. Mike had just joined Tampa Bay and left a message at my hotel room saying he wanted to meet me. When I got the message I thought, "Oh, damn. He finally wants to take me up on that fight now that I'm retired." I didn't know what to think. But I've always been a man of my word and agreed to meet Mike for dinner.

After an uncomfortable hello Mike finally broke the silence. "I know it's been years, but I just wanted to thank you for what happened in that locker room our rookie year," he said. "I was mad for a long time. But that fight made me a better player. You helped me live up to my potential and allowed me to play in the National Football League all these years. So thanks, Floyd."

I tried to act like I expected such a response. But I'm pretty sure my jaw was flapping on the table. I said, "I'm sorry it happened the way it did. I shouldn't have grabbed you. You're a grown man and didn't deserve to be treated that way. I just knew you were a better player than that."

Mike played 13 seasons in the NFL and retired in 1979 after spending a season blocking for my good friend Larry Csonka in Miami. I consider Mike one of the finest players I ever lined up with.

There are many other linemen I want to thank, including George Goeddeke, Larry Kamisnki, Tom Cichowski, Marv Montgomery, Mike Schnitker, Tom Lyons, Claudie Minor, Paul Howard, Bob Young, and Roger Shoals.

NEED CHANGE?

Ohio State's Randy Gradishar was our top draft pick in 1974. He joined the Broncos toward the end of my career and instantly upgraded our defense. At 6-foot-3, and 235 pounds, Randy was the first big Broncos linebacker. He was an intense young man who worked hard from day one. When he retired in 1983, Randy was a seven-time Pro Bowler and one of the leaders of the Broncos Orange Crush defense.

That much is known about Randy, but many fans don't know that he also was a prankster. If something was missing from your locker, there was a good chance Randy was behind it. He could also be a bit of a goof. During one preseason game he saw a quarter lying on the field and called a timeout just so he could pick it up. The rest of the season guys would walk by his locker and pretend they needed to make a phone call. "Randy, you gotta a quarter I can borrow?" we'd ask.

WHOLLY MOSES

After Haven Moses arrived in '72, he went on to play nine incredible seasons for the Broncos. Regrettably, Haven suffered a stroke a few years back, but has now nearly recovered in full. I'm not surprised about his resiliency. He took one of the toughest hits we've ever seen. In a game against the Raiders, he got hit in the helmet, and the blow completely shattered his facemask. It was just dust. Most people would be toe-tagged right there. But Haven got up with only a cut on his lip. "What's wrong?" he asked as we painfully looked back at him in shock.

BA-BA-BARNEY

One of the great, unsung players in Broncos history is defensive end Barney Chavous. Barney was a second-round pick in 1973 from South Carolina State, and played 13 seasons for us. Only John Elway, Tom Jackson, and Dennis Smith were with the team longer.

Barney had a southern drawl that was so thick you could pour it on hotcakes. He also had a stutter, which made for an odd combination. If you think kids can be cruel, try spending some time around an NFL locker room. Everyone had a nickname and Barney's was perhaps the meanest. "Ba-Ba-Barney." He was the one who laughed last.

Barney was surprisingly quick and could rush the passer as easily as he could stop the run. One time against the Raiders he knocked Oakland quarterback Ken Stabler for a bone-crushing sack. Barney got up and nonchalantly tapped him on the helmet for good measure. Stabler got mad and tried to go after him. But Stabler's own linemen held him back.

They knew Barney wasn't the vindictive type. He just walked back to the huddle giggling.

The Broncos have long been a class organization. But back during my era they didn't always handle the dismissal of players with dignity. Barney found out he was cut from the six o'clock news—not the team. After 13 seasons that's how the organization let him go. The team got some bad press about Barney's callous release, so they hired him back as the strength and conditioning coach. I think that made Barney feel a little better, but it was after the damage had been done.

TANKED

The same thing happened to Jim "Tank" Turner. He learned he was cut from a news report in 1979. Jim deserved better. Here's someone who was one of the greatest kickers in NFL history. He kicked three field goals in the Jets' stunning 16-7 upset of the Colts in Super Bowl III and retired as one of the NFL's all-time leading scorers.

He won a lot of games for the Broncos with those high-top boots. The Broncos later elected him into the Ring of Fame, but he's never forgiven the Phipps regime for using the local media to communicate his release instead of telling him face to face. He still lives in Denver and does a lot of charity work but hasn't been involved in any Broncos functions.

TOMBSTONE

Lou Saban blew a few trades in his tenure. But trading for Rich Jackson was not one of them. In '67 he sent Lionel Taylor, who wanted to exercise a clause in his contract to be traded, and another player to the Raiders in exchange for three players that included Rich, who was a backup linebacker at the time. Lou moved Rich to defensive end, and over the next five seasons Rich became one of the most feared linemen in the league. He not only dominated offensive tackles and anyone else who tried to stop him, he annihilated them. The head slap was still legal then, and he devastated guys with it. He earned the nickname "Tombstone," because that's where he would send quarterbacks—to their graves.

Rich loved playing his old team, the Raiders. Whenever we played Oakland he went toe to toe with behemoth tackle Bob Brown. It was like Godzilla against King Kong. We crowded the sidelines to watch them go at it. They hit, shoved, slapped, spit, kicked, and gouged. Hell, they did everything that would garner a personal foul in today's game. It was like watching two bears fight over a lunch basket.

During the '71 season we had the most formidable front four in the league with Rich, Paul Smith, Dave Costa, and Lyle. Pete Duranko also was in there. I don't know where our defense ranked, but I think we were near the top against the run and in pressuring the quarterback.

Rich was battling bad knees and Lyle was a rookie that season. But Lyle adored Rich and worked hard to impress him. And ole Tombstone loved having a protégée, of sorts, to teach. That all changed in '72 when John Ralston took over as coach. He made Rich practice every day on his bad knees, which only weakened them. Then John shipped him to Cleveland for a third-round pick. I don't think Lyle ever forgave John.

SUPER DAVE

Dave Costa may not have been a household name, but he was a super player with a tremendous motor. He was a tough guy—a true character who probably would have fit in well with the Hell's Angels. Dave wore leather jackets, rode a motorcycle, and loved to go out and have fun. Yet despite the tough-guy appearance, he sported a perpetual smile that was evident even when he was mad.

When *Monday Night Football* was born in 1970, the Broncos were still a good four years away from appearing in front of a national audience. It became a point of contention between the team and the league. But instead of focusing on the negative, Dave made *Monday Night Football* a social event. He'd gather a few of us at a pub for dinner to enjoy the game over a couple beers. He was a true entertainer, always cracking jokes. Word got out that he was hosting a *Monday Night* party and more guys showed up every week. Thanks to Dave we became a closer group of teammates, and that friendship lives on thanks to our annual Alumni weekend.

Despite the constant losing, our defensive line remained one of the best in the league. Here All-World defensive end Rich Jackson (87), the great Paul Smith (70), and stars Dave Costa (63) and Pete Duranko (55) make life miserable for the Chiefs' Lenny Dawson. *Courtesy of the Denver Broncos*

SHHH, MR. SMITH

Perhaps the most consistent player we ever had was Paul Smith. He was a quiet guy who was fundamentally sound. Paul wasn't a big talker or a big weightlifter for that matter. But he studied film and perfected techniques that allowed him to become a good pass rusher and an effective tackler. Very few offensive linemen were able to get the best of Paul. He was just too damn good. He'd quietly be among the leaders in tackles and quarterback pressures each game. To young linemen like Lyle, John Grant, and Rubin Carter, Paul was a huge inspiration.

No one ever graded out more consistently than Paul. He's a Ring of Famer who played for the Broncos for 11 years before being traded to the Redskins. He passed away in 2000 and we all miss him.

QUARTERBACK CAROUSEL

Fans and media look back at those Broncos teams during my day and wonder why we didn't win more. After all, we always had a pretty good defense and we were able to run the ball effectively.

I think when you lose there's enough blame to go around for everyone. Even though I contributed in a lot of areas, I was my own toughest critic. When you walk off the field after a loss, you have to look at your own performance first before you can start judging anyone else's. Still, few teams ever win consistently if there is inconsistency in the quarterback position. And that was a glaring problem for us. Until Charley Johnson arrived in '72, quarterback was Denver's Achille's heel. All you have to do is look at how many we had: from 1967-71 Lou brought in 27 quarterbacks.

Lou was an impulsive coach who wouldn't hesitate to pull a quarterback if he threw an interception. Because of that, our quarterbacks were constantly looking over their shoulders. During his first season in '67, Lou made that terrible trade, sending two No. 1 picks to the Chargers for backup Steve Tensi. Because Steve was hurt so often, Max Choboian, Jim LeClair, and Scotty Glacken played, too. The following season Lou brought in several quarterbacks—11 in all—to compete with Steve for the starting job. Talk about a lack of cohesion—every time we ran a play in camp there was another quarterback behind center. We started five quarterbacks that season, which is just insane. Our offense was so out of sync it performed like a car with a shot carburetor.

Finally Lou took a gamble and brought in Marlin Briscoe. As you know Marlin played well, but after one season he wanted to be the highest paid player on the team. Denver didn't have that kind of money and he was gone. The next two seasons, 1969-70, Lou hauled in seven quarterbacks to camp before settling on Tensi, Pete Liske, and Al Pastrana.

Al was a rookie who Lou had coached at Maryland. He was just green. In three starts he tossed eight interceptions. In one game Al was knocked woozy when we were in position for a game-winning field goal. Back then only quarterbacks could call timeout. The game ended with us trying to wake him up to call a timeout.

Pete, on the other hand, had potential. He had played briefly for Lou in Buffalo, then went to Canada and starred in their league before coming to Denver. He was a good leader but forced a lot of bad throws. Once against Buffalo he was sacked five times and threw five interceptions. Lou went berserk. In 11 starts for us, Pete tossed 22 interceptions.

In 1971, Steve Tensi retired, Lou cut Al, and shipped Pete off to Philadelphia. He decided he didn't need all those quarterbacks. He only invited four candidates to camp and traded for Steve Ramsey and Don Horn. Lou was convinced Don was the answer and traded a great, young defensive end, Alden Roche, for him. Alden reminded me of a young Michael Strahan. He was tall, lean, and strong. He had no front teeth, and hence his mouth resembled Dracula's when he smiled. We nicknamed him "The Count."

The first thing I noticed about Don and Steve was neither was mobile. Steve didn't look like a quarterback. He seemed more like the Pillsbury Doughboy. I liked Steve, though. He was gutsy; he just wasn't a great leader. He could never take command of a huddle like Charley Johnson did. Don's problem was just inexperience. In his second game he faced his old team, the Packers, and threw six interceptions. I was standing behind Don near the end of the game and I overheard a coach crack, "Don, you should have told me you were betting on this game so I could get in on the action." Don separated his shoulder a few weeks later against the Bengals, and his short Broncos career was over. Lou resigned the next day, and offensive line coach Jerry Smith took over as interim coach.

When Ralston took over the next season he brought in Charley, but he let Steve Ramsey start the first five games in '72. We went 1-4 over that span. Finally, 34-year-old Charley got a shot to start at Oakland and completed 20-of-28 passes for 361 yards and two touchdowns in our 30-23 win. I caught my first touchdown from Charley and I *threw* a 35-yard touchdown pass to Jerry Simmons on a halfback option. Jerry was such an instigator that I had to kid him. I said, "Jerry, that was a perfect pass. I can't believe you held onto it!"

Charley's performance was the best game by a Broncos quarterback since Marlin's huge game against Buffalo in '68. That game secured Charley's hold on the starting quarterback position, where he remained

Before John Ralston brought in Charley Johnson (middle) in 1972, the Broncos quarterback carousel made winning almost impossible. From 1967-71, Lou Saban brought in 27 quarterbacks. Here are just a handful of them: top row—Scotty Glacken, Jim LeClair, Pete Liske; middle row—John McCormick, Charley, Al Pastrana; bottom row—Steve Tensi, Steve Ramsey, Don Horn; and Marlin Briscoe (pictured on page 78). *Courtesy of the Denver Broncos*

over the next four seasons. Looking back at all the Broncos quarterbacks, one statistic sticks out to me: Of all the quarterbacks we had, only Marlin Briscoe and Charley Johnson threw more touchdowns than interceptions.

TJ

Over the years there were a lot of players who came to me for advice. Because I was captain, some felt I had influence over who stayed and who went. That wasn't true. I just knew what the coaches wanted.

One guy who came to me for advice was Tom Jackson. There's a whole generation of fans who know Tom as Chris Berman's sidekick on ESPN. But Tommy was a great player. At 5-foot-11, and 218 pounds, he was short and light for a linebacker. What he lacked in size, though, he made up for with speed and a ton of heart.

Tommy used to ask me, "What can I do to make the team?" I told him, "You need to go all out on every play in every practice. They never cut you for going 100 percent or being aggressive." I told him that whenever we faced each other in a drill to really go at it. "Don't be afraid to lay me out and do a little shoving afterwards. Make a scene." So one day Tom gave me quite a shot in practice. The team gasped. John Ralston stopped everything and yelled, "Tom Jackson! Hitting our star running back like that is the quickest way outta here!" Tommy thought he had screwed up.

"Did you hear the coach? They're going to cut me," he said afterwards.

"Really," I replied, "what did he call you?"

He looked confused, answering, "He, uh, called me Tom."

"That's right," I laughed. "You're no longer 'Rookie' or 'Jackson.' You're Tom Jackson. They know you!"

When the coaches gathered for the next round of cuts I'm sure they said, "Tommy may be a little out of control, but he goes all out. Let's keep him another week." And that's how you make a team. In fact, John started to keep Tommy out of certain drills along with me. He'd say, "We're going to do the Oklahoma drill. Floyd and Tom, you two sit this one out."

TOM ALL-THUMBS

Tom quickly became a great tackler and eventually a starter. But his "hands" needed work. One time he dropped two easy interceptions in a game. Billy Thompson went over to him and said, "Don't worry, TJ. Stay

Tommy "TJ" Jackson was an extremely quick, aggressive linebacker. At 5-foot-11, he was undersized but had the desire to be great. He also was pretty vocal, much to the dismay of Raiders coach John Madden. *Courtesy of the Denver Broncos*

focused. You can do it." Then, unbelievably, Tom dropped a third easy pick. Billy's mouth opened but nothing came out. Finally he said, "What the hell is wrong with you?"

Later Billy and I teased Tom, "Tom, you trying to catch the ball is like putting perfume on a goat. It's not going to work." Tom, of course, cured his dropsies. During the '77 Super Bowl run he made some huge interceptions, like a 73-yarder for a touchdown against the Colts, and two key fourth-quarter picks in the playoffs against the Steelers.

HEIR APPARENT

When I joined the Broncos in 1967 the average career of an NFL running back was less than two years. As a 25-year-old rookie playing on a last-place team, I knew an injury could end my career at any moment. That's why I played every down as if it were my last.

The Broncos, of course, understood the precarious nature of an NFL running back and prepared each season accordingly. In my nine seasons they drafted 21 other running backs and traded for another six. Of those, one guy eventually became my heir apparent: Otis Armstrong. We drafted him number one in '73. He sat and watched me grind out 979 yards and 13 touchdowns that season while securing my fifth Pro Bowl appearance. During training camp in '74, I injured my Achille's tendon and tried to return from injury too soon. It never healed properly and prevented me from playing with abandon. Otis got the opportunity to start and made one hell of a statement, leading the NFL in rushing, just like I had done three seasons earlier.

Even though I was disappointed with my injury, I took my new reserve role in stride as any professional would do. I always believed the best 11 guys should play regardless of who was on the bench. At 32, I had enjoyed a great career and was among the Top 10 rushers of all-time. But more importantly, as team captain and mentor, it was my duty to make sure Otis was prepared for each game. I told him that talent alone can only get you so far in the NFL. I made sure he worked with his linemen after practice. I coaxed linebackers to stay afterward, too, so Otis could improve his pass blocking.

During the best game of his career, Otis and I got into it a little bit. We were playing the Oilers and Otis had already run for 165 yards and two touchdowns. We were winning 30-14 with two minutes left when Oilers quarterback Dan Pastorini was intercepted by John Rowser. Otis came over to me and said, "Hey, Floyd. Go ahead, take it in. I'm exhausted." Now, I hadn't carried the ball once that day, although I had returned punts and kickoffs. I said, "You want me to go in because you're tired—you mean you're not hurt?" He shook his head. "No, just dead tired. Go in." I said, "Otis, this is what being a starter and a professional means. You keep playing unless you're hurt or the coaches take you out." He again shook his head no. Well, I got mad. I grabbed him by the shoulder pads and pulled him close to me. "Listen," I said. "There's less than two minutes left. We're kicking their ass. This is the fun part. Now go in there and finish the Goddamn job!"

Well, Otis looked at me like, "Old Folks is nuts." Sure, I wanted to play. But during my career you had to break both of my legs and hide my helmet to get me out of a game. I loved Otis, but I wanted to teach him toughness. He went back in and, in a bit of irony, he cut me out of the record book. He gained three yards on his next carry, topping my single-game Broncos record of 166 yards. Then on his final carry he went 15 yards for his third touchdown—tying my team record—for a 37-14 victory.

That's actually one of my proudest memories: knowing I made a young player better without any regard for one of my personal achievements.

7

MONDAY NIGHT MADNESS AND A NEW WINNING ALTITUDE

SURGERY FOR FOLKS

The closest we ever got to the playoffs during my Broncos career was that magical 1973 season. It was the beginning of the phrase, "Big Orange, How Sweet It Is!" Later it became "Orange Crush," until the soft drink company by the same name eventually took us to court to get us to stop using it. If anything, I'm sure we helped their sales—at least in the Colorado market.

Overall, John Ralston's first season as coach in the '72 season had been a disappointment, as we finished 5-9. I had a productive yet injury-plagued season. I played the entire year with an injured knee, but I decided to wait until the season was over to have surgery. I still slugged out 859 yards rushing, 366 receiving, and 13 touchdowns. They didn't have arthroscopic surgery back then; instead they took a huge eight-inch slice down the side.

Since I was 31 the Broncos were unsure of how I would bounce back, John used the Broncos' first pick on Otis Armstrong. He also made a key trade for linebacker Ray May from Baltimore.

HOLDING HANDS

Ray May was probably our biggest addition in '73. He was a savvy veteran who had earned a championship ring with the Colts in Super Bowl V. He also brought with him a unique way of unifying the defense—holding hands. He started it in camp and some guys felt stupid doing it at first. But Ray said it was a way to display unity, to show each other that "I've got your back and you've got mine."

I loved the idea and tried doing it one time on offense. But one of my teammates said, "Folks, watch your hands. Only my wife and girlfriend can do that!"

We won the '73 season opener 28-10 against the Bengals in a game in which I scored three touchdowns. Then we lost three games in a row to the 49ers, Bears, and Chiefs. The hand-holding experiment seemed to be losing its grip.

MONDAY NIGHT MADNESS

Heading into Week 6 we were 2-3 and faced the biggest game in the history of the Denver Broncos up until that point. After four years of being ignored by the national media we were appearing on our first *Monday Night Football* telecast. The whole city was elated. Announcers Howard Cosell, Frank Gifford, and Don Meredith were treated like royalty when they arrived days before the game. The mayor proclaimed the day "Orange Monday." People donned orange outfits, wigs, and made huge signs. The fans wanted to show the nation that Denver was a dynamic place to live with the greatest fans in the world.

The game was on October 22, 1973, and even though Halloween was not for another week, the fans' orange outfits made for a spiritual event. We gave the fans reason to rejoice in the first quarter when Billy Thompson regained momentum for the home team. The Raiders were driving for what seemed like an easy touchdown when Oakland running back Clarence Davis lost a fumble. Thompson scooped it up and raced 80 yards for a touchdown and a 7-0 lead. I think John Ralston ran down the sideline alongside him the entire way. BT was mobbed in the end zone.

But the celebration was short: The Raiders, as usual, came back and methodically scored 13 unanswered points to build a 13-7 halftime lead. When we got the ball back in the third quarter, we went to our basic offensive package of runs, traps, draws, and short passes. We got to Oakland's 10-yard line, and Charley Johnson gave me the ball four straight times before I took it in from the one-yard line to make it 14-13. That carry put me over 5,000 career rushing yards. But I was just happy we had taken the lead.

Oakland had double the yardage we had on offense, and we were fighting our guts out just to stay with them. The whole game was a slugfest. I got clothes-lined on a catch over the middle, and my neck and shoulders began stiffening up as a result. Then, early in the fourth quarter, we tied the game at 20 on another Jim Turner field goal. But Oakland responded, melting the clock down to 41 seconds before the ageless George Blanda booted a 49-yard field goal for a 23-20 lead. With the game almost over, a lot of the Raiders started joking with each other. Some took off their helmets. But we were hardly laughing.

Luckily, we got two breaks. Ray Guy, the Raiders' dependable kicking specialist, knocked two straight kickoffs out of bounds. Back then it was a five-yard penalty and a re-kick. The third time Joe Dawkins returned it to our 38-yard line. Now there was only 30 seconds left. We needed to go at least 20 yards to give Jim Tuner a chance at a field goal.

On first down Charley threw me a quick screen. I dodged two tacklers and ripped up the sideline for 13 yards. With the Raiders suspecting pass, Charley called a draw to Joe Dawkins for 12 more yards. Now with 17 seconds on the clock, the ball was at the 37-yard line with one timeout left. We basically had one more play before we had to let Jim attempt a field goal.

Charley thought about tossing one in the end zone, but needed time to throw. There was always a risk of a sack that would keep us out of field-goal range, so Charley decided to stay the course. "Let's make it a bit closer for Jim," he told us. "Folks, I'm giving it to you, 34 Power Trap. Just put your head down and get us a few more yards and I'll call timeout. Let's do it!"

I hit the hole and there was a nice open spot for me to land. But I saw a crease open behind Mike Current's block, and so I cut back to the right for nine yards. Charley called a timeout with seven seconds left, and Jim knocked a 35-yarder through the uprights for a 23-23 tie.

I know a tie isn't glamorous, but we were happy. We showed a lot of composure coming back against a team known for its comebacks. We were now just 2-3-1, but we were brimming with confidence.

ON A ROLL

Following the comeback tie on *Monday Night Football*, the whole city rejoiced the next day. Neighbors cheered me as I drove to practice, newspapers captured every detail of the game, and I'm told the water coolers were getting extra attention in offices all over Colorado.

The good feelings flowed through every player, coach, equipment person, and staff member in the Broncos organization. We had finally appeared on national television—and we played an inspired game to boot. Of course, the love fest quickly dissolved as it was time for the team to get back to business as we prepared to play the Jets the following week. Leroy Mitchell scored on a 40-yard interception to propel us to a 40-28 victory over the Jets.

The next week we tied the Cardinals, which gave us a peculiar 3-3-2 record. I called a meeting and implored everyone to step up. "Let's get it done this year. I'm not getting any younger," I said. "That's because you're old as shit," a few of them joked. We won the next three games: 30-19 over San Diego; 23-13 at Pittsburgh; and 14-10 at home against the Chiefs, a team we never seemed to beat.

Suddenly we were 6-3-2 but had three tough games left: Dallas, at San Diego, and at Oakland. If we were going to make the playoffs, we would have to earn it.

CHARGED UP

After a tough loss to Dallas, we rebounded with a wild 42-28 win at San Diego the following week. Everyone played well. I scored my 13th touchdown of the season, which equaled my previous season's total. Best of all, the victory raised our record to 7-4-2 and, incredibly, ensured the franchise's first winning season ever.

I'll never forget the reception we got at the airport upon our return. Thousands of fans mobbed us at tiny Stapleton Airport as we stepped off the plane. There were no security people around and the terminals were extremely narrow. I got hugged more times than a newborn baby. It was a circus atmosphere, and after seven seasons it felt great to finally be a winner. We had one game to go: a road game against—whom else—the hated Raiders. The winner would be AFC West champions and go to the playoffs. The loser would go home.

FOR ALL THE MARBLES

The Raiders game began with a bad omen. Prior to the kickoff, hundreds of pigeons were released, I guess, as a picturesque beginning to a championship game. Damn if those pigeons didn't shit all over us as they flew by. Luckily we were wearing white, so it wasn't that noticeable. It just stunk.

Without championship game experience, the team was jittery early on, and the Raiders capitalized with a quick 14-0 lead. Down two touchdowns, our game plan to control the ball with runs and short passes went out the window. By giving up on the run we played right into the Raiders' hands. Their pass rush was among the best in the league and Charley started taking some shots. We managed just a field goal, and by halftime it was 14-3.

Ralston gambled with an onsides kick to start the second half and it failed. The Raiders got the ball in good field position. But our defense forced a fumble and we took over near midfield. It was gut-check time and we responded. We put together an 11-play drive that ended with a beautiful 13-yard touchdown strike from Charley to Haven Moses to make it 14-10. The scored stayed the same going into the fourth quarter, and we felt good about our chances.

That all changed, however, on our first possession to start the fourth. With the ball at midfield, the Raiders blitzed and slammed Charley hard to the turf. He lay motionless for a few seconds. Ralston threw down his clipboard and galloped out to check on his quarterback. Charley was helped to the sidelines with a concussion, and couldn't return to action.

Our hearts sank. It was fourth-and-10 but we still had a whole quarter left. No need to panic. But Ralston felt otherwise and called another fake—this time a—punt. Joe Dawkins was to take a direct snap and hand it off to Otis Armstrong on a counter. Otis wasn't normally in on the punt team and as soon as he jogged on the field the Raiders started pointing at him and yelling, "Hey, he's a new guy!"

We should have called it off. Joe had trouble with the snap and couldn't get it to Otis in time, so he kept the ball and was tackled immediately. Three plays later, Raiders quarterback Ken Stabler found Mike Siani alone for a 31-yard touchdown to give Oakland a 21-10 lead. In less than two minutes we had lost our quarterback and given the game away.

When backup quarterback Steve Ramsey came into the huddle, I could feel the team's confidence disappear. He just stared at the ground when he called a play, unlike Charley, who always looked each of us in the eyes. A few plays into the drive, Steve was picked off by Willie Brown. At that point the game appeared over. Luckily, with only a few minutes left Raiders running back Marv Hubbard fumbled on his own 10-yard line and Pete Duranko recovered it for the Broncos. After I rushed for nine yards on a draw play, Ramsey found Riley Odoms in the end zone for a touchdown, and suddenly the score was 21-17 with three minutes left. The Broncos sideline exploded.

At that point we had nothing to lose and should have tried another onsides kick. But Ralston elected to kick it deep and the Raiders offense ran all but 18 seconds off the clock, and held on to win. We had played valiantly overall but couldn't overcome those costly mistakes. Playing catch-up most of the game, we attempted 38 passes to Oakland's 20. Joe Dawkins and I only ran the ball 10-15 times.

Later in the locker room, a reporter came up to me and told me I had just missed out on 1,000 yards rushing on the season. I just stared at him and shrugged my shoulders. Frankly, I couldn't think of anything less important than another milestone. We had lost, we weren't going to the playoffs, and that was all that mattered.

On the plane ride back to Denver, all I could hear was the engine's low hum. Lyle Alzado, as usual, was sitting next to me, and even he was quiet as a stone. But the somber atmosphere evaporated when our plane taxied on the runway at the airport. We looked out our windows and again saw the fans—5,000 of them—welcoming us home. My eyes welled up. Those fans deserved a playoff team—they were so loyal. As we walked through the terminal they kept chanting, "Wait till next year" and "We love you!" It was incredible.

8

MEMORABLE OPPONENTS

SAY HELLO TO YOUR WIFE FOR ME!

As one of the smallest backs in the league, I learned pretty early on that there was more to surviving in the NFL than merely hard work and taking care of one's self. Running backs were regularly gang-tackled, and so they absorbed a lot of cheap shots. Personal fouls were rarely called back then because the definition of "personal foul" wasn't the same as it is today. Being clotheslined, speared, spit on, kicked in the nuts, and slammed out of bounds was just part of the game in the early '70s. There were no quick whistles, and fumbles weren't analyzed on replays. Any loose ball was a free for all that lasted until the refs felt like interfering.

Due to all these dangers of the game, it paid to be sneaky smart. I tried to diffuse my opponents by getting to know them. The week before each game I would go to our public relations director—Val Pinchbeck and later Bob Peck—and request a copy of the opponent's media guide. No wonder writers loved those things. They contained all kinds of juicy information about a player: how long they'd been in the league; where they went to college; what their hobbies were; even the names of their wives, kids, and pets. Along with studying game film, I used to study the media guide.

The idea came to me the first time I played the Chiefs in 1967. We were getting torched like a paper kite in a brush fire. They were humiliating us 52-9, and their horse, Warpaint, had run up and down the field so many times after touchdowns that he was exhausted. After the final touchdown he just stood in the end zone and took a shit. On one of my final carries of the game, Buck Buchanan—all 6-foot-7 of him— jumped on my back and rode me for five yards downfield before he crushed me into the ground. He made some whooping sound and pushed me into the dirt as he got up. At that point I was already too mad about the game. So I just took it like an old man in prison.

I decided it wouldn't hurt to get to know Buck, as well as some of the other bone-crushing defenders I would have to face on a weekly basis. I read up on Buck in the Chiefs media guide, and before our next game against Kansas City I went over to Buck and said, "Hey, Buck. You know you guys played the Packers pretty tough last year in the Super Bowl. I'm sure you'll make it back soon. Say hello to your wife, Elizabeth, and your three kids for me. Stay healthy!"

I'm sure Buck didn't know what to think. He didn't go half speed during the game, but after the whistle, instead of pushing me into the ground, he'd help me up. We became friends over the years, and it all started because of that media guide. I used the same strategy with guys on the Chargers—including receiver Gary Garrison, whom I met on a US tour to Viet Nam in 1970. I didn't bother with the Raiders, however, because I figured they'd just hit me harder.

KISS MY BUTKUS

Of course, there were some players who didn't go for my media guide routine. One of the all-time greats, Dick Butkus, didn't fall for the banana in the tailpipe. The first time I played the Bears was an exhibition game in 1970. I had met Dick years earlier in '64 with Gale Sayers at the All-America banquets. He was a load of fun off the field. But during the game he wasn't just intense, he was incensed. Yet you would never know that during warmups.

Prior to our first meeting, I went out and patted him on the back and said, "Dick, great to see you. We're finally going to play against each other."

"Yeah, it's about time," he replied. "I'm looking forward to it."

"Me too. Say, how's Helen and the kids?" I asked.

"Oh, they're great," he said.

"Well, good luck, and stay healthy," I told him.

"You do the same, Floyd."

Despite the pregame pleasantries, when the game started it was the same old Dick. He'd curse me after each play. And it just got worse as the game progressed. When he tackled me he'd twist my body to the ground like he did everyone else. Early in the game I stuck my hand out for him to help me up, and he responded, "You gotta be f——ing kidding me. Kiss my ass." Then he stomped back to the huddle. By the third quarter, I had rushed for 137 yards—the last was a 77-yard carry in which I whisked right by him. I could hear him shouting my name all the way down the field: "You're dead, Floyd!" The coaches sat me in the fourth quarter, but Butkus kept looking over at me. At one point he waved for me to come back in. I just laughed and said, "No way."

After the game Dick walked over to me and said, "Good game, Floyd. Have a great season." It was like that cartoon with Wile E. Coyote and the Sheepdog: They'd beat the shit out of each other the whole day, but when the whistle blew they walked home together arm in arm with their lunch pails.

ARE YOU ALRIGHT?

We played the Bears practically every year after the two leagues merged. We faced Chicago again near the end of the '71 season after Lou had quit. Jerry Smith was the Broncos' interim coach and a lot had changed on the Bears' side as well. Gale Sayers had already played his last game, and Dick was suffering from a slew of knee problems. The media speculated that Butkus wasn't the same player, but I didn't believe it. Even at 50 percent, Dick was the best. And in this particular game, I got more carries than ever to find out.

For some reason the Broncos made me the workhorse that game. Usually I averaged about 14 carries a game, sharing the load with Bobby Anderson or another fullback. This time I got the brunt of the carries, 20 or so. In the second quarter I went up the middle and Butkus got a head of steam and tattooed me harder than I've ever been hit. He hit me under the chin and bent me backwards like a soft pretzel.

Now the first rule I taught myself in football was never let the defender know you're hurt. I was in another world, totally disoriented. But I just popped up and hit Butkus on the butt.

"Good play, Dick," I said as I began walking away.

"Floyd, are you alright?" Dick asked me.

"Sure, nice pop."

He continued to stare. "No really, Floyd. Are you sure you're alright?" he asked again.

"Yeah, I'm fine. Why do you keep asking?"

"Well," he replied, "for one thing, you're in *our* huddle!"

I looked around the huddle and saw Dick, Ed O'Bradovich, and Doug Buffone looking back at me. "You're not my teammates," I huffed and put my head down as I returned to the Broncos huddle.

Despite being completely dazed I still rushed for 125 yards—adding to my league-leading rushing total—and we won a 6-3 "thriller."

ME AND MY SHADOW

One of the more interesting—albeit, peculiar—set ups of some older stadiums during my time was the lack of advanced technology. Some stadiums only had electricity on one side of the field, like the old stadiums at Minnesota and Kansas City. So both teams shared the same sideline. Instead of being separated by a field, a table of Gatorade coolers was all that stood between us.

The Chiefs were one of those teams that assigned a spy to attempt to limit my production. The assignment fell to linebacker Willie Lanier. If I was out on a wing, Willie focused on me. If I stayed in to block, Willie kept me in his sights. This even happened off the field. One time after a series I went over to the table to get some Gatorade and there was Willie filling his cup, too. A few series later, I went back and Willie was there again. Finally, I said, "Do you have to follow me everywhere?" He smiled, "Wherever you go, I go." After that I was afraid to duck into the bathroom.

INCENTIVES

No player made a lot of money during my era. So some coaches created financial incentives for players to help motivate them. Of course, depending on what team you played for, the "incentives" were called different things. For example, I was told that the Chiefs defensive players were paid cash "incentives" to keep me under 100 yards.

As my spy, Willie also had a chance to make more than his teammates. So one time when his shoulder pad strap broke and he had to come off the field, I shouted for the coach to call my number. He did and I went right up the middle for 40 yards before Jim Lynch tackled me. "No, no," Willie yelled from the sidelines. Before his pads could get fixed, we called the same play and this time I went for 13 yards. "You son of a bitch," I heard him blare as he finally ran back on the field.

After the game, Willie actually came into our locker room. "How many yards did Floyd get?" he asked our stats guy.

"Let's see, yards from scrimmage, 131; yards rushing, 96," replied our statistician.

"Wahoo!" Willie yelled, jumping up and down. "96—we just made it. Thanks, Floyd."

And he ran out of the locker room a few hundred bucks richer.

INCENTIVES, RAIDERS-STYLE

The Raiders definitely earned their reputation as a bunch of ruthless renegades. We rarely beat them because we always sank to their level. They'd start delivering cheap shots and punch, bite, kick, and scratch, and we'd do the same in retaliation. They didn't try to tackle me as much as try to maim me. Instead of tackling me, guys would try to hold me up—so their buddy could take a shot at me. They'd even pull my arm out to expose it so that someone could ram a helmet into it.

The Raiders' aggressive style brought out the worst in us. We often sunk to their level, but always played them tough. Here I am running past Otis Sistrunk (60) in the '73 season finale. Jerry Simmons (80) is looking for someone to hit while my old teammate, Nemiah Wilson (48), takes in the action. *Courtesy of the Denver Broncos*

One of my best friends during my career was Raiders defensive back Nemiah Wilson. He was on the Broncos before joining Oakland, and we became good friends. He still lived in Denver in the off-season and we went into a tailoring business together. We also trained together by running the steps of Mile High Stadium in combat boots.

Nemiah shared with me one of the secrets to the Raiders' success. Each game they had bounties placed on certain guys, and I, of course, was given the highest bounty. He told me they had a guy whom they called "The Spiff Coach" who paid them in cash after every game. A "spiff" is a term for a cash payment based on an incentive. The players would line up and say, "I knocked Floyd Little out for two series," or "I gave Charley Johnson a concussion," and the "Spiff Coach" would hand over an envelope containing hundreds of dollars.

One time against the Raiders, I was running a trail pattern behind tight end Riley Odoms. Riley ran a crossing pattern behind the linebackers and I trailed five yards behind. It was Charley's job to hit the open guy. I made my cut and had just obtained a bit of an opening when I looked over and saw Riley a step ahead of the linebacker. Charley threw a perfect pass and Riley made a fingertip grab. Raiders safety Jack Tatum came up and knocked the snot out of him with a helmet-to-helmet lick. Riley landed on his back and was out cold, but somehow he held on to the ball. Jack, as usual, stood over him to enjoy the moment. I looked at him and thought, "Shit, that could have been me." Tatum, no doubt, received a nice payday after the game.

Money motivates, and the Raiders were the proof. I tried to protect myself as best I could against Oakland. But as a running back, there wasn't much I could do.

NOT TODAY, FAT MAN

Raiders coach John Madden was an amusing guy to watch. He waved his arms like a maniac during games, and always wore a short-sleeved shirt, even when it was minus-20 degrees. It's amazing that he never caught pneumonia. He also kept his field credentials dangling from his belt loop so security knew he was allowed on the field. As if they didn't know who this 6-foot-5, 260-pound coach was.

But what was so funny about Coach Madden was his every-guy persona. Guys treated him like a fellow player and loved to trash talk him. You never saw opponents teasing Saban. Madden, however, was fair game. Surprisingly, the top trash talker on our team was Tom Jackson. On TV broadcasts nowadays, Tom is the most courteous, professional guy. But as a player, Tommy was one of the biggest loudmouths, and no one talked more trash to Madden than Tommy. The Raiders would try some double reverse and Tommy would stop it for a loss. Instead of jawing at some of the Raiders, Tommy would turn to Madden and say, "Not today, fat man! You're going to sweat some weight today." John hated listening to Tom, too. "That Tom Jackson never shuts up," he used to say.

WHO TOOK MY CLOTHES?

Another tough linebacker I played against was Mike Curtis of the Baltimore Colts. Mike went all out on every play till the whistle blew. One time I was running around the left end and passed the first-down marker. I looked up and had no lane to cut back, so I was forced to go out of bounds. Well, Curtis came out of nowhere and just leveled me. He hit me between my shoulders and helmet and I went flying out of bounds. I was out cold. When I finally woke up I was naked on the shower floor. I don't know how I got there and worse, I don't know who took off my clothes. I was just thankful I wasn't naked in the Colts' shower! I learned an important lesson that day: never presume you're not going to get hit.

TAILS, YOU LOSE

Considering how much we hated the Steelers as a team, it's a bit odd that I became friends with a number of Steelers. I played in Pro Bowls with Joe Greene, Jack Ham, and Andy Russell, and I even knew the voice of the Steelers, Myron Cope, from his reporting days. This friendship continued for years when we all participated in Andy Russell's annual golf tournament.

Of those players, I'm probably closest to Andy. Yet, there's one thing that I did to Andy that still angers him to this day. As team captains we were out calling the coin toss before a Broncos-Steelers game. The referee, Tommy Bell, said, "Captain Little, this is Captain Russell. This side of the coin is heads, this side tails. Captain Little, you make the call."

I thought for a second, and as Bell flipped the coin I joked, "Heads we win, Tails you lose." As the coin hit the ground, Bell looked at Andy and said, "Tails you lose, Captain Russell. Okay, Captain Little, do you want to receive?"

Andy was furious. He said, "Wait a minute. What's going on here?" He tried arguing with the referee, trying to show him that I had confused him. But the longtime referee was either embarrassed or didn't believe him. He just shook Andy off and told him to return to his side.

That whole game Andy tried to get back at me. Because of our friendship we never wanted to embarrass each other. He used to give me a heads up if he was blitzing. His function was not to get to the quarterback, but to keep me from going out in a pass pattern. In this game, though, he gave me false signs. He would pretend he was going to blitz and instead he'd break out into coverage. After a few plays I went over and asked him, "Why are you so mad?" His response was short but sweet: "Kiss my ass. You f—-ed me, now I'm going to f—k you."

Even today, we can joke about most things. But he still gets mad if I bring up that coin flip.

SON OF STRAM

I played in an era with a lot of memorable, talented coaches. One of the best was Hank Stram. We rarely beat his Kansas City teams, and many times they flat-out killed us. The fans sure as heck hated the Raiders, but the Chiefs were our real rival. We really respected them, and the few times we beat them gave the team a huge lift.

I was in the locker room putting on my uniform prior to one meeting against the Chiefs at Mile High. As I went to grab for my No. 44 jersey, I realized it wasn't there. I asked the equipment manager what the deal was, but he claimed that he put out my jersey. We quickly determined that someone had stolen it. While an assistant drove back to the practice facility to get another one, I went out to warm up wearing No. 46.

As I went through calisthenics and began fielding punts I looked over, and Stram was fiercely staring at me. Suddenly, I felt this presence behind me. I turned and Stram was two feet away.

"Who are you?" he said, trying to see past my facemask.

"Huh? I'm Floyd Little, Coach."

"Floyd Little?" he said. "You're wearing No. 46. You've got the wrong jersey on."

"I know. Someone stole my jersey," I replied.

He looked at me and a smile broke out. "Whew, for a second I thought you guys had a secret weapon," he said.

The irony is I found out years later that Stram's son was the one who stole my jersey. I was in Kansas City giving a motivational speech, and he came up to me and confessed. "I was a big fan of yours as a kid and wanted your jersey," he told me. He apologized, and also admitted to stealing Joe Namath's helmet once. I started laughing. Maybe Hank got his kid to steal "memorabilia" from opponents so they'd lose focus before games. You never know.

COACH STRAM TO THE RESCUE

In my nine NFL seasons, I played the Chiefs 18 times. So I got to know guys like Buck Buchanan, Willie Lanier, and Bobby Bell quite well. We bonded at the Pro Bowl, before and after games, and during off-season charity events.

Due to that bond, a particular play against the Chiefs in a 1972 game at Arrowhead stadium stands out in my memory. It was a brutally cold day and I had rushed for about 90 yards by the end of the third quarter. Snow was swirling around, and the wind chill made the temperature feel like minus-25 degrees.

I was handed the ball on an off-tackle play near the goal line, and after a few yards linebacker Jim Lynch wrapped his arms around my thighs to try to bring me down. Meanwhile Curley Culp, a former teammate of mine, had his shoulders wedged between my legs. I tried to lunge forward when defensive end Marvin Upshaw stuck his helmet under my chinstrap, knocking me backwards. The impact forced my legs apart like a wishbone. I could feel my cartilage tearing, and I reacted with a blood-curdling holler. Buck and Jim saw what was happening and pulled Marvin and Curley off of me, yelling, "Stop!" Unbelievably, it worked. Everyone let up.

As I began to fall to the ground, a couple Chiefs grabbed me and kept me from landing awkwardly. I looked over and the coach was running to my aid. Not our coach, John Ralston, but Hank Stram! He got there first. The game was held up for five minutes to make sure that I was okay. In fact, instead of my teammates, it was Stram and a couple of the Chiefs who helped me to the sidelines where I sat for the final quarter.

Ralston told me he had never seen a player garner so much compassion and respect from the opposition. "We've faced the Chiefs a lot," I said. "We respect the hell out of each other." After the game a number of Chiefs stopped by our locker room to see if I was okay. Of course, Willie also wanted to check to make sure I hadn't gained 100 yards, too.

THIS LITTLE PINKY'S NAMED FLOYD

Over the years I've played in a lot of charity golf tournaments. At one such tournament in Arizona I ran into Earl Edwards, a former defensive tackle with the 49ers. He looked at me and blurted, "God damn, it's Floyd Little. You son of a bitch!" I was taken back. I only played San Fran a few times in my career, so I had no idea why he was giving me a hard time. "Look at my finger, Floyd. You see what you did?"

Turns out the first time we played them he got his pinky caught in my shoulder pads while trying to tackle me on a long touchdown jaunt. His finger was bent like one of Chuck Bednarik's mangled digits. It looked like a protractor. He said, "You know what I call this finger?" I shook my head. "I call it my F——-ing Floyd Little Finger!" he said. "Every day when I look at that twisted pinky I think of you, dirty bastard."

I was touched!

KEEP YOUR CHIN UP, SWEETNESS

Not all of my post-playing day encounters were quite so odd. One that sticks out—for a positive reason—was the time I met young Walter Payton. It's hard to believe, but there was a time when the great Payton was an up-and-coming running back trying to make a name for himself. It was the last game of the '76 season, and I was announcing a Bears game for NBC with my favorite colleague, Ross Porter. After the game, Bears general manager Jim Finks came up to me and asked me to talk to their young running back, who had just lost the rushing crown to O.J. Simpson.

"Floyd, this kid is really dejected about losing the rushing title," Finks said. "You've led the league. Could you please talk to him and let him know he'll be okay?"

"Absolutely," I said, following Jim into the Bears locker room. There, sitting by himself near his locker, was Walter, head down, slowly getting dressed. I said, "Hi, Walter. I'm Floyd Little." Walter looked up and his eyes brightened, "It's great to meet you, Mr. Little." I continued, "I just want you to know I think you're a great young player. Don't get discouraged about the rushing title. Remember, this is just one season. I've heard you're a hard worker, a dedicated guy. That's going to take you a long way. When your career is over I wouldn't be surprised if you hold all the records."

He smiled. "Thank you, Mr. Little," he replied. "That means a lot." Knowing that Walter went on to accomplish so much, I'm honored that I had the chance to give him some encouragement.

9

MORE MEMORABLE GAMES AND PLAYS

INSULT TO INJURY

Even though I finished with 729 yards rushing during the 1969 season, it could have been an even bigger year than when I led the NFL in '71 with 1,133 yards. I was in my third season with our young offensive line, and we were starting to build a cohesive rhythm. They understood the way I ran, and I was learning to be more patient. In '68 we showed glimpses of greatness, like when I gained 147 yards against the Patriots and 126 yards versus the Dolphins and my buddy Larry Csonka. I started the '69 season with back-to-back 100-yard games, and I was gaining an average of over 6 yards a carry. I followed that up with over 130 yards from scrimmage against the Chiefs and another big day against the Raiders. After five games I was the NFL's rushing leader despite missing a game due to injury.

Then we played Cincinnati in Week 6 at tiny Nippert Stadium, and I had my biggest day as a pro. Our offense moved the ball at will that day. I'd gain 5, 10, 20 yards on the same play run consecutively. I always felt the secret to breaking a long run was to run the same play over and over.

Even if you don't make many yards the first two times, you see how the defense reacts, then *swoosh*—you're gone.

I had that kind of day against the Bengals and capped it off with a 48-yard touchdown run after setting up the defense with the exact same play on the previous down. I rushed for 166 yards that game, and suddenly I was more than 300 yards ahead of every back in the NFL. I was on pace for a 1,400-yard season.

Unfortunately, the next week against the Chargers I got hit in midair and landed awkwardly on my knee. I was in a cast and missed five games. It took that long for San Diego's Dickie Post to overtake my rushing total. But Gale Sayers beat him out in the end with a total of 1,032 rushing yards. He was the only back that year to gain 1,000 yards.

Sometimes I think "What if?" about that '69 season. But injuries are a part of the game. You play every play like it's your last, because it might just be.

RUNNING SMARTS

Throughout my career I always played hurt. Running backs get hit so much you have to be able to distinguish the difference between pain and injury, or you'll never suit up. A few times, I crossed the line and played when I should have been laid out on the operating table. The 1970 season was one of those times. I had broken the transverse process bone in my back earlier in the season; it was the most painful injury I ever had. Yet somehow I played all 14 games that season and, even though I wasn't at full strength, I led the AFC in rushing with 901 yards. I would have reached 1,000 with more touches, but I carried the ball just 209 times.

My best game that year was against the 49ers at old Kezar Stadium. They had a phenomenal team and just missed the Super Bowl that year, losing in the NFC title game to the Cowboys. Playing a great team was all the motivation that I needed. I scored on an 80-yard carry in the first quarter by punching through a hole on the left side. I cut across the field to the right and no one could catch me. By halftime I had over 100 yards rushing and finished with 140, even though we passed most of the fourth quarter before falling short, 19-14.

VICTORY SNATCHED

It may seem strange to have a game you lost remain so vivid in your mind, but our '72 home game against the Minnesota Vikings is one of those games that affected me like few other. It was a game in which we had no business winning. Then when we grabbed the lead near the end it appeared like there was no way we could lose.

The game had special motivation for me. Clint Jones, the first running back taken in the '67 NFL draft was starting for the Vikings. I had nothing personal against Clint. I had met him at Bob Hope's All-America TV special and liked him. But I constantly wanted to prove to people who doubted me that I was the better pro. The other motivation for me was the thrill of battling the relentless Vikings defense, known as the "Purple People Eaters." I always believed a player tested himself against the best. That's how a player knows if he's any good.

By the second quarter the Vikings were winning, 6-0. We had done little offensively, so the next series coach John Ralston made a switch at quarterback and Charley Johnson took over. Charley marched us down the field. With a critical third-and-3 at the Vikings' 36-yard line, Charley changed the play from a run to a quick-screen to me. I caught the short pass and weaved through a handful of tacklers, turning on the afterburners for a 36-yard touchdown. We went into the half confidently ahead, 7-6.

Then in the third the Vikings took control and scored 10 points to pull away 16-7. It looked like a typical Broncos game for us: We stayed close for half the game, then watched the game slip away. But just when all seemed lost, we recovered the ball on a turnover, and I turned in one of the better runs of my career.

I took a handoff deep in the backfield and cut up the middle, eluding defensive tackle Alan Page. I was met by linebacker Roy Winston, who grabbed my jersey and held on for a couple yards. I did a 360-degree spin and cut back to the outside. Then I traversed across the field for the final yards and the touchdown. I think all 11 Vikings had a chance to tackle me at one point in my carry. I must have zigzagged for twice the yards during this 27-yard carry. The play cut the Minnesota lead to 16-14.

53 seconds to glory. In this '72 game against the Vikings at Mile High, I'm engulfed by teammates after scoring my third touchdown of the game to take a 20–16 lead with less than a minute left. Seconds later Minnesota scored on a long pass for a shocking 23-20 victory. It became one of the most haunting losses in Broncos history. *Courtesy of the Denver Broncos*

We got the ball back with 7:27 left in the game and put together an incredible 12-play drive. It was perfectly executed, and I could see the Vikings players becoming frustrated. I finished the drive off with my third touchdown of the game to give us a 20-16 lead with just 58 seconds left. The Mile High crowd was going nuts.

The Vikings needed a miracle. They found one by the name of Francis Asbury Tarkenton. Fran quickly moved the Vikings 63 yards in 45 seconds, completing three-of-four passes in the process. The last was for 31 yards to Gene Washington, who beat a hobbling Randy Montgomery for a dramatic, game-winning touchdown with just a few seconds left.

I was speechless after the game. It was the first time where I felt like I couldn't have done anything more to help my team win. I scored three touchdowns, gained 100 yards on 18 carries, and had another 40 yards receiving. Usually with a loss I'd walk off the field thinking, "I could have gained one more yard, or made one more block." This time was different. I sat with my head in my hands in the locker room for almost 20 minutes.

I was upset because my best wasn't good enough. I remember yelling to no one in particular, "What do we have to do to win around here?" It was perhaps the most bitterly frustrating loss of my career. I was told afterwards that Vikings coach Bud Grant kept repeating, "That Little is some back!" My one small consolation was I outgained Clint Jones 100 yards to 7. But he left Mile High Stadium with a win, and I didn't.

ONE-YARD WONDER

It seems crazy, but one of the best touchdowns of my career was a 1-yard run against the 49ers. We were in one of those shootouts at Mile High during the 1973 season. Late in the game I got the ball on a straight dive play. I was supposed to go inside Marv Montgomery's block, but instead his opponent got past him, and Marv inadvertently pushed him into me. I quickly bounced to the outside and was hit at the 3-yard line by the 49ers Pro Bowl cornerback Bruce Taylor. He tagged me hard underneath the shoulder pads and began to push me back.

I bent my legs, lowering my torso closer to the ground, and started pumping my feet. It was a test of wills, two No. 44s fighting for the end zone. No one was within five yards of us. Slowly I started to gain an advantage, but Taylor continued to fight. I pushed him back to the 2-, the 1-yard line, and finally lowered my shoulder and drove him into the end zone.

My teammates say it was the darnedest thing they ever saw. I went from losing three yards on the play to scoring a clutch touchdown to give us a 34-33 advantage. I was engulfed by my fellow Broncos in the end zone. Predictably, the 49ers kicked the winning field goal minutes later.

HEE-HAW!

Except for that Vikings game (which still stings), I try to focus on the wins. In my nine seasons the Broncos went a paltry 47-73-6. But every

Sometimes making a play comes down to a test of wills. In this '73 game at Mile High, 49ers Pro Bowler Bruce Taylor hit me at the 3-yard line, but I managed to carry him into the end zone for a fourth-quarter touchdown. Despite the short run I consider it one of my best touchdowns. *Courtesy of the Denver Broncos*

once in a while there were games that we not only won, we dominated. One of those games came in 1971 against the Browns in Cleveland.

The game had all the signs of a classic upset. The Browns were a perennial playoff team. A couple years earlier during the merger talks, Browns owner Art Modell made the comment that his Browns would never play in a losing AFL city like Denver, and that he certainly wouldn't allow "those Denver Donkeys" to come to his grand Municipal Stadium. Coach Lou Saban had saved all those comments and tacked them on our bulletin board prior to this game. Lou, after all, was a former Browns star, and so he took great offense.

Our passing game was nonexistent at that point, so Lou's philosophy was simple: "We're going to ram the ball down their Goddamn throats," he roared before the game. And that's what we did. It was a perfect day for smashmouth football—overcast, rainy, and with plenty of mud. We ran the ball 30 times in the first half to build a 24-0 lead. The Browns couldn't stop us on offense, and our defense was superb. We intercepted three passes and held the Browns' entire running game to 24 yards.

By game's end we had rammed the ball down their throats to the tune of 280 rushing yards. I gained 113 of those yards and sat out the fourth quarter. Bobby Anderson notched another 70 for us, and my backup, Fran Lynch, pounded them for 50 more.

I even got in a wrestling match with 265-pound Browns defensive tackle Walter Johnson. He wouldn't let me up after a run and we started going at it. Fred Swearingen was the official, and I think he loved watching a little guy get the best of a big guy. He didn't even throw a flag.

By the fourth quarter we were up 27-0, and it started pouring. The Browns had no recourse but to try to pass, while we continued to knock the snot out of them. The 27-0 victory was the first time the Browns had been shut out since the early 1950s, a span of 274 games—an NFL record. We were yelling, "Hee-Haw!" at them. This great playoff team was thoroughly embarrassed at home by the Denver "Donkeys."

I don't know how we got home safely after that game. We were jumping up and down on the plane and racing up and down the aisle. Our pilot, Joe Murphy, was no doubt nervous. It was the first victory in a long line of huge wins for us over the Browns. Fittingly, it also was Lou Saban's last win as Broncos coach.

10

MILE HIGH SENDOFF

THE FINAL SEASON

Looking back on my final season as a Bronco in 1975, I'm still amazed that it ended on such a high note. At 33 years old, I was ancient for a running back. My painful Achille's injury forced me to surrender the starting job to Otis Armstrong the previous season, and as the '74 season came to a close I told coach John Ralston that I would come back for one more year and do whatever the team needed me to do. I was happy to play special teams and return kicks—I didn't care.

I trained just as hard in the off-season prior to the start of the '75 campaign, but I was no longer mentally focused on starting, which caused my whole mindset to change. That's why when I hear athletes teetering on whether they want to play another season, I know that mentally they're already shutting down.

I figured I'd carry the ball maybe 15-20 times the whole '75 season. I was already among the Top 10 all-time rushers, so I didn't care about adding to my total. I went through the first few games in '75 returning kickoffs. In the third game we felt we could run the screen well against the Bills, so I came in and scored on a 35-yard play. I jogged off the field satisfied in knowing that I had just scored my last NFL touchdown. Then Otis tore his hamstring the next week against the Steelers and was done for the year. Suddenly, I was back in the lineup. It took me a few games to get back to the mentality of being a starter.

We played the Chiefs in Week 6 and I rushed for 70 yards. Then we played the Bengals two weeks later, and I had 90 yards from scrimmage and a touchdown. A couple weeks later against the Falcons I totalled 120 yards from scrimmage and had well over 5 yards a carry. Mentally and physically, I was playing as well as a 30-plus year running back old could perform. Unfortunately, our injury report was mounting. We were losing more and more guys and more and more games.

PREGAME EMOTIONS

By the time I suited up for my final home game at Mile High Stadium against the Philadelphia Eagles in Week 13, we were a disappointing 5-7 and had lost a dozen players to injury, including six starters, the biggest being quarterback Charley Johnson.

The week before the Eagles game I began receiving a slew of cards and telegrams from former players and coaches. Local and national sportswriters wrote articles about me. Dolphins linebacker Nick Buoniconti sent me a great article written about me by *Miami-Herald* writer Edwin Pope. I think Dick Connor of the *Denver Post* and Chet Nelson of the *Rocky Mountain News* also wrote a column a day about me.

But the majority of the well-wishers were fans. Many of them thanked me for representing the Denver Broncos so well for nine seasons; some thanked me for saving the franchise; others simply told me that I was their hero and a true role model for kids. It was an emotional week for an emotional guy. I'm a Cancer in the Zodiac world, and Cancers cry watching cell phone commercials. *Brian's Song*? Forget about it—I need 12 dozen tissues.

THE FINAL GOOD-BYE AT MILE HIGH

As I was introduced for the final time to the home crowd, I remember marveling at the stands being filled despite the frigid 18-degree weather.

It was a week before Christmas and we weren't playing for anything, but the fans were bundled up and cheering like it was opening day. They had brought along all kinds of signs. One of them had my face on the body of Superman. Another read, "No one can ever replace our 'Little' gap." My eyes were already welling up, and the game had yet to begin.

When I got to the sidelines before the game, I was hugged by Billy Thompson, Charley Johnson, Fran Lynch, Lyle Alzado, Rick Upchurch, and the rest of the team. A couple of Eagles, Harold Carmichael and Bill Bergey, ran over to wish me good luck. "The NFL will miss you," Bergey said to me.

The game had a magical atmosphere. Snow had fallen and flurries continued throughout the game. By halftime we were up 10-7, thanks to a Jim Turner field goal and a touchdown by my roommate, Fran Lynch. I had gained only 12 yards, but any butterflies I had endured before the game were long gone. Coach Ralston decided that we were going to start the third quarter by running the ball. Jon Keyworth and I ran the ball seven times in a row before Billy Van Heusen had to punt. The touches helped me settle in and feel comfortable.

Near the end of the third quarter, the game was tied 10-10 and we had the ball on our own 34. At this point we were having fun in the huddle. The guys were yelling for quarterback Steve Ramsey to run plays behind them. "Give me Folks," they'd say. "Let Folks run behind me. I'll carry his geriatric ass." A screen pass play came in from the sidelines, and I immediately became excited. I said, half-joking, "Hey, this is a great play. Make your blocks, because I'm taking it all the way." The funny thing was that deep down I believed it. Throughout my career I always excelled at screen plays. Many of my touchdown receptions came on screen passes, which gave me the space I needed for my cutbacks.

The thing I remember about catching Steve Ramsey's perfect floater was that my linemen were still behind me. I teased them about it later. After catching the ball I was like a scuba diver in shark-infested waters. I had Eagles coming after me from all directions. I made a couple guys miss, then Billy Van Heusen threw a great block and Haven Moses moved out in front to lead me down the right sideline. When I got to the 30-yard line several Eagles had an angle on me, so I cut back to the inside and headed for the goalposts. The last Eagle dove at my legs around the

10-yard line and missed as I galloped into the end zone. The touchdown went for 66 yards and I was mobbed by my teammates. The noise at Mile High climbed an additional 10 decimals as we took the lead.

Later in the fourth quarter I scored again from two yards out on a sweep to make it 25-10. Bill Bergey helped me to my feet in the end zone and said, "Great game, my friend." After a rather pedestrian beginning to my final home game, I finished with 150 yards from scrimmage and two touchdowns.

As the final minutes of the game ticked down, I lost it. When you're drowning they say your whole life passes in front of you. Standing on that sideline, I could identify with the sentiment. As the two-minute warning sounded, I realized my career was finally coming to an end. I just stared at the clock and my teammates. I had been playing football since I was a kid, and now I was 33 years old and looking down the end of my career. Mentally, I was ready to leave the game. Physically, I could have played longer. I could have chosen to stick around and pad my stats like some running backs have done, but I was never about the yards or the records. I cared most about the game, about winning and doing everything I could for the good of the team.

In those final few moments, Coach Ralston put his arm around me and tears streamed down my face. There's a great picture of that moment that hung in the Pro Football Hall of Fame (and is included in this book). Alongside that photo is a second picture—which appears on the cover— of me being carried off the field that day on the shoulders of two burly fans. That was surreal. I've seen coaches and players carried off a field by teammates, but never by fans. That was the single greatest moment of my career and it came at the very end. To be carried off the field by the greatest fans in the world in my last game at Mile High Stadium is something I'll cherish until the day I die.

In the locker room after that great moment, every player and person in the Broncos organization congratulated me. Players and coaches were asking for my chinstrap, shoes, elbow pads, you name it. I happily obliged. I was the last to leave that locker room that day, and as I walked out a limousine pulled up and out popped Charley Johnson dressed as a chauffeur. "Your car, Sir," he said. Inside sat my wife. They had planned a farewell party for me at a nearby hotel. It was an extravagant affair with

In my final game at Mile High Stadium, I scored two touchdowns, including an exciting 66-yard touchdown off a screen pass. Overall, I accounted for 150 yards from scrimmage. As the clock wound down on my career, coach John Ralston congratulated me, as my emotions got the best of me. Moments later I was carried off the field by the great Denver fans. *Photo by Barry Staver*

coaches, players, and wives in attendance. They even prepared an ice sculpture carved to resemble my No. 44 jersey. We all stayed late laughing and talking about the game and the funny things that had happened over the years.

The person who really stood out for me that day was Charley. Here was a guy who was probably the most underrated quarterback of all-time. People didn't realize that this, too, was his final game at Mile High Stadium. He played 15 great seasons in the NFL and was the epitome of a professional. He should have been sharing the limelight with me. But instead he humbly and unselfishly took a backseat. Charley was just an amazing person for doing that. Today he continues to be one of my best friends.

MIAMI, NOT-SO-NICE

People forget that even though that memorable game at Mile High Stadium was my last home game, there was still another game to play the following Saturday at Miami. As it turned out, I wish the game had never been played. We lost to the Dolphins 14-13 when, in typical Broncos fashion, Jim Turner's game-winning field goal attempt was blocked. Charley Johnson was the holder and I felt horrible that his last play was spent running after a loose ball.

Meanwhile, I had stood on the sidelines for most of the game after twisting my ankle early in the second quarter. Charley, sore shoulder and all, was told he could go in for one play at quarterback to hand off. "Nah," he said, "I'd probably try to throw long."

11

POSITIVELY OLD SCHOOL

SHOES, GLORIOUS SHOES

Recently I took a tour of the Broncos facility at Dove Valley. Boy, oh, boy was that impressive. The players have everything you can imagine. Three outdoor practice fields: one with grass, a second one that is heated, and a third field with the latest carpeted turf. There's also an indoor field covered with that new plush "Field Turf." Off the field, there's a fully catered cafeteria, a brand new weight room, a training room with three large whirlpool baths, players lounges, game rooms with Web hookups, a sweet locker room, and separate meeting rooms for every position including larger rooms for team meetings. There was even an old photo of me in the training room. I just want to go on record saying I wasn't in the training room all that much!

I'm sure every team in the NFL has a similar setup. But I can't imagine any of them nicer than the Broncos. I'm proud to see how far the organization has grown over the years. I know some of the things seem unnecessary, like game rooms, but I think that's to keep the players around one another as much as possible to increase bonding. Obviously our training facility in the late '60s and early '70s was nothing like that.

It was more like a series of huts—like where'd you go if you were given detention.

The one thing about Dove Valley that stood out most to me was the shoes. Every player seemed to have a dozen or so different pairs of shoes. When I played, we only had one pair! We wore the same cleats in practice as we did for games. We just washed the dirt off them. If the field was soggy, we didn't change into longer cleats. We unscrewed the shorter cleats and screwed in the longer ones. Seeing all those shoes reminded me of an episode of *The Simpsons* where Marge is in New York City and she's mesmerized by a line of new shoes in a store window. "Wow, look at all the shoes," she gazes, "too bad I've already got a pair!"

SPECIALISTS GALORE

As I was winding up my career, the NFL was already changing. There were some running backs in the league who were becoming "specialists." The Colts had a guy, Don McCauley, who was used in that role. He'd come in the game on third downs and was usually the main target on a swing pass or some draw.

I was asked if I'd consider coming back as a specialist. Since I never considered myself a part-time player, I declined. I'm sure if I would have agreed I could have extended my career by a few years. I may have even played in the Broncos' first Super Bowl in '77. Or I could have played for another team. But I had always been a Bronco, and I wanted to remain a Bronco. I didn't want to play for anyone else, and I definitely didn't want to pad my totals as a role player. I take great pride in that I was an every-down back, and I was still returning kicks in my final game. John Madden said he admired me because I could run, catch, block, and return kicks. And Jack Ham called me the most complete back he ever played against.

Now you've got third-and-5 guys and short-yardage guys. Everyone's a role player it seems. Case in point: I'm the last Broncos running back to have a 100-yard receiving day. (I collected 127 receiving yards versus the Chargers in '74.) That's significant.

A RUNNER'S GAME

I would love to carry the ball in today's NFL, especially as part of the Broncos' zone blocking scheme. Very rarely do you see a back without a clear lane and, even better, a backside lane to cut back. The reason is simple: today's game involves more finesse. Our linemen couldn't use their hands. They went helmet to helmet and blocked with their shoulders and arms, not with their hands. They couldn't extend their arms. Today it's all about positioning and technique. You can basically hold; it's just the interpretation of holding. You see guys hook their hands and arms around players' outside shoulders and move them to an area. Linemen in our era had to keep their hands and forearms close to their chests like priests.

It's tougher for defenders to stop offenses these days. When I was tackled it was usually up around the neck or helmet, which probably shortened my career and made me a few inches shorter. Fortunately, they changed the rules, and now you can't tackle that high. But you can't really play bump and run against receivers, and you can't even lay a lick on the quarterback anymore.

Moving the hash marks to midfield changed the game a lot, too. That happened in '72 after I turned 30 years old. It provided offenses more room to either side. Willie Lanier said it made his job as a middle linebacker tougher because he had to cover more space. It also was the first rule change that favored backs, increasing the number of 1,000-yard rushers. In '71, when I led the NFL in rushing, I was only the 13th back in history to gain 1,000 yards in a season. Then in '72, they moved the hashmarks closer to midfield, and 10 rushers reached the 1,000-yard mark.

More records went out the window in 1978 when the regular season was extended from 14 to 16 games. Then in the early 1980s, Redskins coach Joe Gibbs went to a one-back offense so he could have an extra blocker to combat the likes of Lawrence Taylor. Teams followed suit, and suddenly fullbacks were no longer splitting carries, they were just blocking. Tailbacks went from carrying the ball 200 times a season to well over 300 and sometimes 400.

That's why it's so hard to compare eras. We played under a completely different set of rules, and every year it seems the NFL gives offenses more advantages, because people like to see touchdowns, not great defensive struggles. I'd love to see the NFL reinstitute some rules to help the defense. Can you imagine an announcement like, "In order to halt the excessive holding by offensive linemen, we're bringing back the head slap!" I think old Tombstone—Rich Jackson—would scramble to go find his helmet in the attic.

THE NFL'S BLACK EYE

Baseball is no longer our national pastime. Football has replaced it and continues to be the greatest game in the world. The NFL is the only league that does it the right way with revenue sharing and a salary cap. The only guaranteed money a player receives is his signing bonus. The rest he has to earn. I think fans like that approach because they can relate to it. That's how the real world works.

Still, guys are able to earn incredible incomes as NFL players. They don't have to work in the off-season like we did in my time. And the NFL makes about $2 billion a year off television revenues, ticket sales, team apparel, and so forth. As former players, we helped pave the way for this amazing level of prosperity. We sacrificed our bodies and our well-being by playing in the most violent sport of them all. Yet our health benefits and pensions are dramatically less than those in any of the major sports. It's become the NFL's black eye.

I've been lucky. I got out of the game when I was relatively healthy. I didn't wait around for the NFL to take care of me; I worked hard outside of football for 30 years to achieve financial security. But many of my former teammates have not been so fortunate. They've got serious financial problems and do not have the money to pay for mounting health care costs as a result of injuries sustained during their playing days. Many have crippling diseases. Remember Johnny Unitas a few years back before he passed away? He was the NFL's greatest quarterback who grew the sport in the 1950s. He had to have both knees replaced, and he couldn't even pick up a fork with his throwing hand because three of his fingers didn't work. But when he needed money to cover these expenses the NFL turned its back on him, citing some stipulation that he didn't file until after he was 55 years old. It made me sick.

I think with all the money the NFL makes, a portion of it should go to retired players to help cover health-care costs. I don't think it's too much to ask. We were the generation that helped build the league, the ones who didn't make a lot of money. Our life expectancy is only 58 years, a good 15 years below the national average. Many of us are divorced. Some have battled alcohol and drugs. Still, we're directly responsible for the success of the league. Every year each team gives $1 million to the NFL's legal fund. But since Al Davis seems to be the only one who sues the NFL, there's probably a great deal of that money available. I think a portion of it should be given to help aid former players.

The sad truth is a lot of people have gotten rich from the NFL—but not our generation.

NFL CODE

There is a code in the NFL about being a professional. I believe it still exists today despite all the talk by some current players about "being entertainers." Regardless of our record, my teammates were dedicated to working hard each week to improve the team. We took our status as professional athletes seriously. We worked hard to be prepared for each opponent and gave it our all. Players who dogged it in practice, who forgot plays and didn't go all out, did not last in the NFL. When I saw guys quitting in practice or in the fourth quarter, I didn't want to play with them anymore. Luckily, most of my teammates upheld that code. They played with character and pride. They were incredible team players who cared about one another.

No matter the score, I always looked at how we played in the final quarter. Who went all out until the final whistle? It's an attitude that I always sought out in opposing players, too. Players simply collecting a paycheck were not respected.

If there was one thing players in the league knew about me, it was that I went all out. I played every play as if it were my last—even in preseason. During one exhibition game against the Colts, our rookie punt returner was injured. No one would go on the field to replace him, so I grabbed my helmet and returned a punt 89 yards for a touchdown. I was in my 30s then, and people made a big deal that a "star" would volunteer to return a punt during a "nothing game." But that's simply what I got paid to do.

Guys around the league respected me. They'd tell me, "You never quit." That meant more to me than any of my Pro Bowls.

12

THE FINAL, FINAL GAME AT MILE HIGH

SUPER FAN

In the 30 years since I retired from the NFL, I've continued to be a diehard Broncos fan. I became a season ticket holder after I retired, and was at Mile High with other Broncos fans when we won those two spectacular playoff games against the Pittsburgh Steelers and the Oakland Raiders in 1977 to reach the Super Bowl and square off against the Dallas Cowboys. I even stood in line in frigid 10-degree weather to try to get Super Bowl tickets, but came up empty. The Broncos didn't give me any tickets and the team only allocated so many to season ticket holders, so I waited in line like everyone else. Fans couldn't believe it. One guy said, "If Floyd Little can't get Super Bowl tickets, how the hell can I?" and he just left. The Phipps owned the team then and even though they were good owners, they didn't always treat former players well.

After I retired I was hoping to get a job with the Broncos in some capacity. But they never offered, and I was too proud to ask for one. Other teams called the Broncos and asked if they could talk to me, to which they replied, "Sure." I got offers from the Seahawks, the Giants, and a few others. I was offered a job with the NFL, but it meant moving to New York and negotiating with team player reps. As a former rep I wasn't comfortable doing that. Besides, the Broncos were the only organization I wanted to work for.

I did some research and discovered that the Broncos were the only team at that time that hadn't hired any of their former players. It upset me so much that I left Denver. I thought if I couldn't work for them, I'd pursue other work. So I moved to Los Angeles, and continued working for Coors and Ford—companies I had been employed with in Denver. Eventually I quit Coors and opened a Ford dealership in Santa Barbara, California. I've been a Ford dealer for the past 16 years in Federal Way, Washington, about 30 miles south of Seattle.

Since Pat Bowlen became the owner in 1984, things have improved 180 degrees for former Denver players. He developed the Ring of Fame to honor former players and has enthusiastically embraced the alumni network. I think he's the greatest owner in the NFL.

SHUT UP AND EAT YOUR HOTDOG

After missing out on the Broncos' first Super Bowl, I went to Super Bowl XXI in Pasadena, California, and sat with Sam Brunelli, my former teammate, and Jack Kemp, the former Bills quarterback and senator. We were sitting in the end zone when the Broncos had that first-and-goal at the 1-yard line before halftime. We tried three runs and lost yardage each time, then we missed a chip-shot field goal.

Before the last play, a sweep to the left side, I knew we weren't going to make it. I could see it in the linemen's eyes as they walked up to the line of scrimmage. They had no confidence in the play. I remember thinking, "Why are we trying a sweep? We just need a yard." I was getting ticked. My competitive juices were flowing. I started shouting, "Give me the damn ball. I'll get that yard. I don't even need linemen." Jack started laughing, knowing all too well about my intense playing days. Sam just shook his head. He told me to shut up and eat my hot dog. "Folks, you can't play anymore," Sam told me. "You're 44, and I'm not talking about your old jersey number."

He was right, but it didn't make watching the Broncos lose to the New York Giants any easier.

WE WON?

I went to see the Broncos face the Washington Redskins in San Diego for Super Bowl XXII in 1988, and was in New Orleans for the brutal loss to the San Francisco 49ers in Super Bowl XXIV in 1990. That's what made Super Bowl XXXII the greatest sporting experience of my life as a fan. Even if you're not a Broncos fan, if you saw the reaction on the Broncos bench when linebacker John Mobley knocked away that last Brett Favre pass to secure Denver's first world championship, then you had to get goose bumps. Personally, I wept like a baby. The Broncos were something like 12-point underdogs in that game against the Green Bay Packers, the epitome of NFL supremacy during my era.

You couldn't have written a better script for John. As a 15-year veteran who was 0-for-3 in previous attempts at a championship, John received perhaps one last shot at glory against the reigning Super Bowl Champions in the same city where he had lost the big game 10 years earlier.

Once again I attended the game. But this time the only reason I needed someone to hold me down was to keep from floating away. Like a lot of fans and former Broncos players I felt like I, too, had finally won a Super Bowl. Terrell Davis had a game for the ages as did the entire Denver offense, defense, and special teams. All the loyalty and frustration we had endured over the years came pouring out of us in an eruption of utter joy, especially since we won so dramatically at the end.

I think fans and former Broncos had to pinch themselves at that moment, as John was carried off the field amidst streams of confetti and fireworks. I didn't sleep a wink that night. I remember catching ESPN later in the evening and seeing a misty-eyed Tom Jackson, prouder than the NBC peacock. Chris Berman gave a champagne toast to Tom and Broncos fans everywhere.

The Super Bowl victory the following year against the Atlanta Falcons was great, too. It further validated the Broncos as one of the true marquee teams in the NFL. But that first championship was a true thrill, the culmination of years spent in pure devotion to a team.

BLOWN AWAY

I have only a few heroes: Jim Brown, Ernie Davis, Michael Jordan, John Elway, and my son, Marc. I got to know John Elway after his rookie year in 1983 when the team sponsored a Broncos cruise for fans. I spent time on that cruise getting to know then-current Broncos like John, Keith Bishop, Dave Studdard, and Steve Watson.

We had a good time and visited different ports during the trip. At one stop, we saw an advertisement for parasailing. This was 1984, when parasailing was at its height of popularity. I wanted to try it but I was—and still am—afraid of heights, so I declined. A few of the younger Broncos were ready to do it, too—until the parasailing instructor casually announced that the waters were shark infested. I was thinking, "If John decides to do it—we owe it to the organization to pick him up and throw him back in the boat before he puts the parachute on."

The thing I liked right away about John was that he treated everyone the same. He made a point to get to know not just me, but many of the former Broncos. He was hounded by the media to the point where they were reporting on what kind of candy he gave out at Halloween. But it never affected his performance on the field. He had the best arm I'd ever seen, and he made plays that a robotic quarterback wouldn't be able to execute.

John and I became friends. He got into the car business after me, and we used to give each other a hard time about who was the better salesman. Whenever I hosted a charity event John would graciously sign a few items for me. And I'd participate in his golf tournament each year. I know he respected me as a former player, but I never knew how much until after the Broncos beat the Packers in the Super Bowl.

During his golf tournament that spring I was told to stop by his hotel room for an impromptu party he was throwing. I came into the room, and John spotted me and managed to work his way through the large crowd to say hello. He gave me a hug and thanked me for being a pioneer in the Broncos organization. I looked around like, "Is he talking to me?"

He said without my impact on the franchise the Broncos would never have remained in Denver. I was shocked and speechless, which is unbelievable because by now you know I can talk! My glasses looked like they just went through a car wash. I was so overcome with joy that all I remember saying in response was a few words of thanks, before I ran out of the room before I flooded it with my tears. Boy, oh boy. I'll never forget that moment. In my mind John's the greatest quarterback of his era, greater than even Dan Marino and Joe Montana.

THE FINAL, FINAL FAREWELL

I had mixed emotions when the announcement came that they wanted to tear down Mile High Stadium. I understood that the stadium was over 50 years old. But it was still the shrine where all that Rocky Mountain magic happened—usually as the sun began to set and the sky was emblazoned orange.

Everyone remembers all those incredible last-second, John Elway-orchestrated comebacks there, but I held similar memories from my playing days. I had arguably the greatest—and the worst—game of my life at Mile High against Buffalo. I set a Broncos record with 295 combined yards and still got fired by coach Lou Saban. It was also the scene of the infamous "Half-Loaf" game, the first Monday Night game in Broncos history, the NFL's first overtime game, and my final home game where I was carried off the field. After I hung up my cleats, the Red Miller "Orange Crush" Broncos continued the magic at Mile High.

I've been to Invesco Field at Mile High a number of times. It's a magnificent facility, and I'm sure all the corporate suits enjoy the view and the delicious cuisine from their luxury suites. Heck, I even came back to campaign for the new stadium to help get the deal passed. But when I look out the window on the outside of Invesco Field and see where Mile High used to stand—that hallowed ground now a parking lot away—it saddens me a bit.

FIELD OF DREAMS

As big of a treat as it was for the fans to watch some of their legendary Broncos play one final game—albeit a flag football game—at Mile High against NFL legends like Joe Montana, Roger Craig, Dave Krieg, and William "The Refrigerator" Perry, I think it was an even bigger thrill for us players. It was surreal to be reunited with teammates like Billy Thompson, Rick Upchurch, Randy Gradishar, Riley Odoms, Haven Moses, Louis Wright, Barney Chavous, Bobby Anderson, and Steve Foley. And it was like an out-of-body experience to line up with younger guys like Mark Jackson, Vance Johnson, Craig Morton, Karl Mecklenburg, Dave Studdard, Keith Kartz, and, of course, John Elway.

The thing I'll always remember about that week of practice was catching footballs from John. I couldn't believe how hard that guy could throw. And he was retired! Steve Watson used to joke about the "Elway Cross"—how he would throw the ball so hard that the point of the ball would leave a cross-impression on receivers' chests. When I heard that I thought, "Well, you're not supposed to catch the ball with your chest, you're supposed to catch it with your hands." I quickly learned that to do so was impossible with John's passes. I thought perhaps the best way to catch passes from him was to let the defensive back try to catch it first and then grab the pop up.

The finale was a fun game of sandlot football. We diagrammed plays in the huddle and teased each other unmercifully. There was plenty of gamesmanship, wisecracking, and even smack-talk amongst the players. Imagine an older guy like me talking smack with a "young" guy like Everson Walls? He must have been like, "Old man, drink your Ovaltine."

Even though I was the oldest guy there I may have surprised a few people. I could still play. I had participated in charity flag football games in recent years, playing in the Margarita Bowl in Phoenix with guys like Tony Dorsett, Billy "White Shoes" Johnson, and Jim Plunkett. With two minutes left in the game I experienced John's last two-minute drill ever. Down 27-26, John threaded a nice 15-yard touchdown pass to me to pull us ahead 32-27. I remember it was the same end zone I had scored my final touchdown as a Bronco. We went for two and, just like in Cleveland during "The Drive," John completed the pass to Mark Jackson. Then

One of the biggest thrills of my post-football career was playing in the Mile High Farewell game in 2001. I joined John Elway on his final drive at Mile High, scoring the winning touchdown in our 34-33 victory. *Courtesy of the Denver Broncos*

with about a minute left, the NFL legends scored on a long pass and went for two to win. Even with the game on the line we were laughing on the sidelines as they lined up in the Wishbone. "Where's Barry Switzer?" I joked. They fumbled the ball and we ran out the clock to seal the victory.

I'm honored to say that I got the final carry at Mile High Stadium, taking a handoff from John's 12-year-old son, Jack. The final score: Broncos legends 34, NFL legends 33. We all stayed on the field as fireworks went off overhead. It was the perfect sendoff for a grand, old stadium.

13

THE WORLD'S GREATEST FANS, THE WORLD'S GREATEST GAME

STANDING UP FOR THE BRONCOS

After leading the NFL in rushing in 1971, the Pro Bowl rosters were announced. I figured several Broncos deserved recognition: Rich Jackson, Dave Costa, and Billy Thompson on defense; and offensive linemen like Larron Jackson and Mike Current. After all, I couldn't have led the NFL without the help of my line. To my shock I was the only Bronco selected, and even I was just an alternate. How was that possible? I was disgusted. I checked the AFC roster, and the Chiefs had nine players represented, the Dolphins and Colts each had seven selected, and the Raiders added six more. No team had fewer Pro Bowlers than the Broncos.

At the Pro Bowl luncheon before the game, Bob Lilly and I were there to represent the two conferences. The national press only asked Bob questions, ignoring me the entire luncheon. Finally, the host said, "Thanks everyone, for coming," then looked over and saw me. "Oh, wait a minute," he said. "We've got Floyd Little here from the AFC. Floyd, do you have anything to say?"

The Broncos never received the national press we deserved. I was the only Denver player selected to the Pro Bowl in 1971. Despite leading the NFL in rushing, I was just an alternate. I made my displeasure known at a pregame press conference, then helped the AFC win in the fourth quarter on this 6-yard touchdown run.
Courtesy of Floyd Little

Some media had already left, but I got up and said, "Well, that's about right. Once again the AFC has gotten no respect—especially the Denver Broncos. I can't believe I'm the only Bronco chosen by the media. This is supposed to be the Pro Bowl—the best players from each team and conference. There are nine Chiefs here, and one of them—my friend Buck Buchanon—has been hurt most of the year. The Broncos are so disrespected we've never even been on *Monday Night Football*."

One reporter said we hadn't been featured on Monday night because Mile High Stadium didn't have any lights, which was a lie. "Have you ever heard of an away game?" I replied. My tirade went on for another five minutes as I passionately defended my team.

The next day the headlines read, "Little wants to be traded." A reporter had taken everything I said out of context. The Broncos front office got some calls and even a few of my teammates believed the story. But some guys like Larron Jackson defended me. "C'mon," he said, "this is Folks. He loves us. He would never say those things."

That night I was supposed to accept the award for Pro Athlete of the Year from the Colorado Sports Hall of Fame. I was afraid to go because I thought I'd be booed. Bob Peck, the Broncos public relations director, told me that people who knew me realized it wasn't true and, if anything, this was the perfect forum to set the record straight. I was afraid of what I might say to defend myself. I had a colorful speech all prepared just in case. But when I walked out to accept the award, not only did no one boo me, I received a standing ovation that lasted five minutes. People were chanting, "We love Floyd!" I was about to cry. I had never been so surprised in my life.

Bob looked at me and said, "See, I told you."

A DAY IN MY HONOR

I always knew the Broncos fans and the city of Denver appreciated the way I stuck with the team for my entire career. They could always count on me to play my heart out no matter the score. They also admired my community work, which was something that came natural to me. I had to overcome many obstacles as a child, so I have a special attachment to kids. I still make speeches to high schools in the Seattle area, where I now live. Of course, first I show them a video clip of my days with the Broncos, so they know a little bit about this stocky, bowlegged, older gent standing in front of them.

When the city of Denver honored me with Floyd Little Day on October 29, 1972—for both my impact on and off the field—I was so taken aback that I felt like royalty. The announcement was made at the Broncos Quarterback Club luncheon the week after we suffered a wretched last-second loss to the Vikings. It was one of the best pick-me-ups of my life.

A ceremony was held at Mile High Stadium before a game against the Cleveland Browns. I was given all kinds of incredible gifts from friends

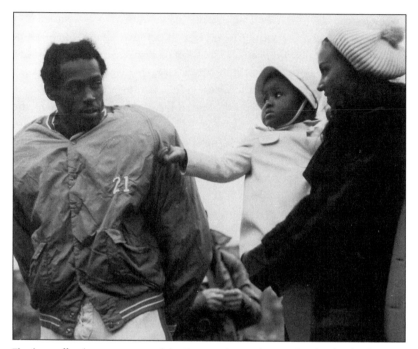

The love affair between me and the Broncos fans culminated with "Floyd Little Day,"
held October 29, 1972, at Mile High Stadium. Here I'm no doubt speechless as I
take it all in with my former wife Joyce and my daughter Christy.
Courtesy of the Denver Broncos

and teammates. I made a speech thanking the fans and looked over at my
wife and baby girl, Christy, and my eyes, of course, began to well up. I
was grateful for the ceremony and the opportunity to thank the great
Denver fans.

The game that day was emotional, too, because Rich Jackson had just
been traded to Cleveland, and I knew he wanted to give me a special
"hello" smack. On one play Rich had a chance to grab me on a quick
screen from Charley Johnson, but I cut past him and scored on a 19-yard
catch and run. On the way back I smacked him on his ass, "You missed
me!" He laughed and said, "You dirty dog."

In the years following Floyd Little Day, I was recognized nationally for
humanitarian service and awarded the YMCA's Brian Piccolo Award in

1973, as well as the prestigious Byron "Whizzer" White Award in 1974. I also was the first Bronco to have my No. 44 officially retired, and was among the first class inducted in the Ring of Fame. All of those honors meant a lot to me, but none meant more than Floyd Little Day.

THE FANS

I hope Broncos players never forget the reason they're able to put on a uniform and play in the great city of Denver: the Broncos fans. Owner Pat Bowlen doesn't really pay their salaries; the fans do when the purchase tickets, merchandise, and memorabilia. Broncos fans are the most passionate, loyal group in the NFL. Many of them have been season ticket holders since 1960. Some have passed away and the tickets have been handed down to new generations of fans. Watching the Broncos on Sundays is a heartfelt ritual the entire city and the state of Colorado embraces.

In my era the bond between fans and players was special. We weren't rich athletes like today's players; instead we were well-paid working-class people. That fostered a neighborhood atmosphere throughout town, where we were very public figures. We didn't live in mansions or drive around in expensive cars. We worked in Denver during the off-season, selling cars or life insurance, working construction, or running small businesses.

The fans loved us, and we loved them. Even if we lost by 30 points, our fans would still cheer, "You'll get 'em next time!" There was always a crowd waiting after games. Fans wanted to get our autographs or give us a hug or just pat us on the back. There was no greater honor than to play for a city where every time I pulled on my jersey, laced up my cleats, and grabbed my helmet and ran onto that field I felt like I was at the center of the universe. The fans respected us, and for that I'll always be grateful.

SELLING THE SIZZLE

As an owner of a car dealership I learned a long time ago that you don't sell the steak, you sell the sizzle. During my years with the Broncos I did a lot of advertising for different businesses. I did endorsements for

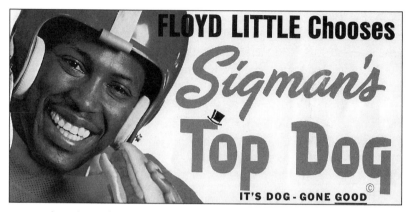

I enjoyed my share of endorsement deals in the Mile High city. Here is the infamous billboard that my teammates loved to tease me about. *Courtesy of Floyd Little*

TV commercials, radio, and print, and my face was plastered on billboards all over Denver. One billboard my teammates teased me about was for Sigman's Hotdogs. The ad was a close-up of me wearing a helmet without a facemask and holding a hotdog. The billboard read, "Floyd Little Chooses Sigman's Top Dog. It's Dog-Gone Good." Of course teammates chided me, saying, "Folks is so old he don't even wear a facemask."

Another ad was for Day Chevrolet in which I actually sang, "Any day you can beat a Day Deal that'll be the day!" For some reason, I never won a Grammy.

WRONG LITTLE, PART I

As a sports hero in a sports-crazy town, I experienced my share of imposters. One guy used to frequent this singles club downtown and tell women that he was Floyd Little. My wife even got a call from another woman at 2 a.m. who was trying to rat me out. "I just want to tell you that Floyd is here at this bar talking to three women, and it doesn't look like he's leaving anytime soon." My wife looked over at me in bed and said, "Floyd is right here. Good night."

Before coming to Denver, Val also was the public relations director at Syracuse. He was a trusted friend and advisor, but was also perhaps the person most responsible for me becoming a Denver Bronco. We remained good friends for years. A few years ago he finally retired from the NFL and moved to Florida with his companion, Joanne Parker, years after his wife Panzie passed. Of course, someone with Val's knowledge and instincts were hard to come by. So the NFL office called Val up frequently for advice, to help with schedules and brainstorm ideas. In March of 2004, Val was in New York doing just that when he suffered a heart attack while crossing a street. He was immediately hit by a taxi and died instantly. It was a huge personal loss for me, as well as countless people throughout the NFL.

A memorial service was held for Val a month later in New York at Saint Paul's Cathedral. There must have been 1,000 people in attendance. It was a Who's Who of the NFL, including NFL Commissioner Paul Tagliabue and NFLPA president Gene Upshaw. Giants great Frank Gifford, a good friend, spoke at the service. I took my son, Marc, because I wanted him to know about one of the great people who influenced my life. There isn't a time when I think about my Syracuse and Broncos days that I don't think about Val and what he meant to me. He was one of the greatest men I ever knew. He will be missed.

NOT SO FAST

At least once a week a fan comes up to me and asks me why I'm not in the Pro Football Hall of Fame. The most embarrassing time was in Pittsburgh when I was at a charity event for a children's hospital, seated at a table with Joe Greene, Jack Lambert, Jack Ham, Mel Blount, Deacon Jones, and broadcaster Myron Cope. This kid came up to me and said, "Oh my God, six Hall of Famers at one table. That's got to be some kind of record." I said, "Not so fast. There's only five. I'm not in the Hall of Fame." A few of the Steelers looked at me in shock. "Really, you're not?" they asked. "No," I said, "I've never been nominated." The Steelers players couldn't believe it, and neither could the kid. I couldn't believe how bad I felt.

WRONG LITTLE, PART II

Have you ever purchased a lottery ticket and thought for a minute that you were the big winner? That same feeling happened to me about 15 years ago. I was at charity event in Los Angeles and some supporter recognized me and yelled, "Floyd Little! Congratulations, I just heard the great news!" I said, "What are you talking about?" He told me, "You've been elected to the Pro Football Hall of Fame. It was on the radio." I was flabbergasted. "Really?"

I was smiling so much I was almost panting. Then I thought, "Wait a minute, is this really true? No one even told me I was nominated." So I called a buddy to check it out. He said, "No, man. You didn't make it. They said, 'Larry Little,' not Floyd." It was as if someone jammed his fist down my throat and ripped out my heart. I try to laugh about it now. But damn, that was upsetting.

WHY NOT ME?

When I retired in 1975, I was considered one of the top running backs of my era. The Pro Football Hall of Fame Selection Committee voted me to the All-Pro Squad of the 1970s. They hung a large plaque in the Hall in Canton, Ohio, commemorating my career. For years after my retirement writers mentioned me in articles as "Future Hall-of-Famer Floyd Little." But I'm still waiting for the "future" to arrive; since my retirement, I've been overlooked.

In 2005, 30 years after playing my final game and tired of constantly fielding questions from fans and former players, I decided to look for some answers. I asked the powers that be—the nine Seniors Committee members who vote for the old timers—why I've been overlooked. I sent personal letters to each of them. Plus I sent a note to Paul Zimmerman of *Sports Illustrated* because he's one of the 39 overall voters, and I regularly catch his insights on the *Sports Illustrated* Web site. Of the 10 votes I sent letters to, only three replied: Zimmerman, David Goldberg, and Edwin Pope.

Through my correspondence, the writers told me they're asked to consider only two criteria in evaluating a running back's candidacy:

"Yards rushing and Super Bowls." That's it. Pro Bowls, receiving yards, combined yards returning punts and kickoffs, impact to your team and the league, years captain, and overall reputation are not given much weight. So I checked out the criteria for the Baseball Hall of Fame in Cooperstown and it was totally different: "Voting shall be based upon the player's record, playing ability, integrity, sportsmanship, character, and contributions to the team(s) on which the player played."

The difference in the criterion for HOF induction between these two major sports is intriguing. Has football's criteria always been this shortsighted, or has it changed since the Hall opened in 1963? And what kind of message does it send to kids who dream about someday being inducted into the Pro Football Hall of Fame—that character, sportsmanship, leadership, integrity, reputation, and community work don't matter as long as you've got great stats and played in a Super Bowl? I'm not spewing sour grapes. I seriously think it's something the Hall of Fame committee should re-evaluate, because I know the NFL prides itself on positively influencing children.

Now that I've been informed of the basis for candidacy, my lack of Super Bowl appearances continues to be a strike against me. But, really, is there a running back who could have willed the 1967-75 Broncos to a Super Bowl? Like a lot of positions, I think running backs play a role, but there's a lot that goes into a championship team. You have to have a great owner, a superior coaching staff, a winning system, a smart general manager, talented players on both sides of the ball, and a good deal of luck. I think when it comes to Hall of Fame selection, too much emphasis is put on Super Bowls. It's one game. What about a player's entire career?

During my prime, from 1968-73, I led the NFL in both rushing and yards from scrimmage. Heck, in my nine seasons, only O.J. Simpson rushed for more yards. Then consider that I came into the league as a 25-year-old rookie, played for a perennial losing team, was the Broncos' only real offensive threat for most of my career, played special teams, and still became the seventh all-time rusher. I think my numbers speak for themselves.

A few years ago Marcus Allen was a first-ballot selection to the Hall after he retired seventh on the NFL's all-time rushing list. I've learned that

There's been great debate as to why I'm not in the Hall of Fame despite retiring as the NFL's 7th all-time rusher. Even though it's a sore subject for many who follow the Broncos, the Denver media has had some fun with the Hall of Fame's snub. *Courtesy Drew Litton and the Rocky Mountain News*

all running backs ranked seventh in 1980, '85, '90, '95, and 2000 have all been inducted. And the six guys ahead of me when I retired: Jim Brown, O.J. Simpson, Jim Taylor, Joe Perry, Leroy Kelly, and John Henry Johnson got in years ago. So why not me?

My 6,323 career yards still ranks in the Top 15 of the 39 Hall of Fame running backs. Even though my numbers may not compare with today's backs, the selectors understand it's an unfair comparison. Ball carriers today tote the rock almost twice as much as backs did in my era. In 1970, I led the AFC in rushing with 901 yards on 209 carries. In 2000, Edgerrin James led the NFL with 1,709 yards on 403 carries. It's impossible to compare the eras by looking only at raw numbers like the accumulation of yards. Just imagine how the stats of today's runners will measure up with NFL stars 30 years from now in the year 2036? It's all relative.

Each year my chances continue to dwindle, but I still have hope. I realize the writers who vote for the Hall of Fame have an incredibly tough job. I appreciate their task and realize they vote based upon the criteria the Hall has established. I'm grateful to those who have passionately spoken on my behalf. Yet, I still think I belong in the Hall. Sure, there are a lot of deserving players out there. But, I think when you look at my production and overall impact to the Broncos, I'm as worthy as any. I was a trailblazer who, along with the Broncos' great fans, helped keep this organization going when the club could have easily folded. Plus, I've got the numbers to boot.

John Mackey, the legendary Colts tight end, once sent a letter to the selection committee requesting my induction. He so eloquently wrote, "If there's no room for Floyd Little in the Hall of Fame, please take me out and put him in. He deserves it that much." That's a significant tribute from a Hall of Famer who played in my era. I still keep a copy of his letter in a drawer in my office.

I think being immortalized in the Hall of Fame is the greatest honor. It's a tribute the fans and the entire Broncos organization can share. Right now John Elway is the only Bronco in the Hall of Fame. We're too good of an organization to have just one player in the Hall. I'm getting up there in age at 64 years old. The life expectancy of NFL players is 58, so I'm already on borrowed time! I just hope if my name is called I'm not staring down from above. I want to be here to dance with my family, teammates, and the great Broncos fans.

LOOSE ENDS

There are more stories and anecdotes to be told, but these tales are the ones that impacted me the most. Playing football for the Denver Broncos was the greatest time of my life. I had the best teammates and played for the greatest fans in the world. Yes, we suffered through some of the toughest times in Broncos history. But there were so many incredible times as well. Times that I continue to cherish every day. I gave it everything I had for nine seasons. I think my teammates and fans know they got my very best effort each and every time out. The game doesn't owe me a thing. I'm glad I had the opportunity to play the game for as long as I did.

One thing's for sure, as a former Bronco and Syracuse alumni, I'll always bleed orange.

ACKNOWLEDGMENTS

There are so many people I'd like to thank it would take me the entire book to mention them all. So I will try to keep it to people who directly helped me put together this book. Thanks to Doug Hoepker and Mike Hagan from Sports Publishing; my man BT—Billy Thompson—and his lifelong friendship; Jim Saccomano, Rebecca Villanueva, and the entire Broncos organization; my friends at Syracuse, Daryl Gross, Sue Edson and her staff, Roosevelt Rick Wright, Larry Martin, and my friend and teammate, Gary Bugenhagan. I'd also like to thank two people whom I have enormous admiration and respect for— John Elway and Jim Brown. Your words, generosity, and friendship mean the world to me. Thank you.

In addition to Billy Thompson, I'm still close to my former teammates, especially Jerry Simmons and Rich Jackson, plus several guys from my Syracuse days. I also remain close to plenty of people from the Denver and Syracuse communities, my hometown of New Haven, Connecticut, and my current home in Seattle, Washington. But my family is my heart and soul—my wife, siblings, nieces, nephews, and especially my children. Of all my accomplishments on the football field, nothing means more to me than my life off the field with my family.

All three of my children graduated from college, are extremely successful, and happily married. That, I believe, is the proper standard which should be used to judge the success of a parent. My youngest daughter, Kyra Little DaCosta, is probably the most talented of my kids. A Broadway performer who toured with Bette Midler, she can sing, dance, and act with equal aplomb. A true triple threat! My oldest daughter, Christy Little Jones, is a great talent also. Besides being the mother of my three grandchildren—Skye, Blaze, and Hayes—she is the family's historian who keeps us together. She plans our family's activities and has a giant heart. She attended Syracuse as well as American University. I'd be remiss if I didn't thank my first wife, Joyce, whom I spent 20 wonderful years with, for sacrificing her own personal pursuits to help raise such incredible daughters.

Then there's my son, Marc Little. He's a lawyer in Los Angeles and my best friend. We talk almost every day. If we miss a day, we notice it. He's a special gift that was given to me later in life. When I was at Bordentown, I fathered a child out of wedlock. About 25 years ago I was home visiting my mother in New Haven when I saw him as a young man. He was 15 at the time, and the resemblance was eerie. No DNA test was necessary: He was my son.

In 1987, while attending college at USC, Marc was held at gunpoint during a robbery and shot in the leg. He was rushed to the hospital and flat-lined a couple of times. His leg had to be amputated, but somehow through the grace of God he pulled through. When I learned he was going to be okay I said to him, "If you don't make it, can I have your TV?" We have that kind of a joking but loving relationship. He's my hero. When I finally grow up, I want to be like him.

Many years after my divorce to my first wife I met a beautiful woman named DeBorah Green at a Syracuse function, and we married in April, 2003. She is so stunning that friends kid me that "I've out-kicked my coverage." DeBorah is a Godsend who is even more beautiful on the inside. She's very supportive and loving, and she's one of the most positive people I've ever met. She travels the country as a motivational speaker. If you thought this book was inspiring, you should listen to her for an hour! She's made my life very enjoyable, and we laugh about something every day. Buddies nudge me and say, "Where can I get me a DeBorah?" I'm just glad I found one for myself.

—Floyd Little

This book could not have been completed without the hard work, patience, and generosity of the following people: Doug Hoepker, John Humenik, Noah Amstadter, and Mike Hagan of Sports Publishing; Rebecca Villanueva and Jim Saccomano of the Broncos for their contributions above and beyond; the Broncos media and marketing departments; Sue Edson and the public relations staff at Syracuse University; Doug Ottewill and *Mile High Sports Magazine*; the *Denver Post* photo department; Ander Murane and Drew Litton of the *Rocky Mountain News*; Jim Rydbom of the *Greeley Tribune*; Larry Felser of *The Buffalo News*; Barry Staver for his incredible photographs; Rich "Tombstone" Jackson for unknowingly fixing my golf swing; Billy Thompson for his humor and generosity; Kathy Hatch for her consummate professionalism. Plus, I'd like to extend a special gratitude to John Elway and Jim Brown for their thoughtful, gracious words. Thank you to you all.

Finally, I'd like to thank the man himself, Floyd Little, for his enthusiastic, tireless dedication to this book. You think it would be difficult to coordinate hundreds of hours of interviews with a legendary player who lives 3,000 miles away on the west coast. But Floyd made the process effortless and immensely enjoyable. For six months every Tuesday and Thursday we discussed personal recollections of his life and playing days. He told me stories and anecdotes that were so funny and touching I couldn't help but end each call feeling inspired and moved. Floyd continually gave of his time with unbelievable candor, passion, and generosity.

If I needed an old press clipping, letter, or photo, he would overnight it to me immediately. Floyd Express was faster than Federal Express or any other delivery service. Aside from his enormous heart, Floyd's greatest trait is his integrity. If he says he's going to do something, he does it.

His family was equally supportive. When I attended the No. 44 retirement ceremonies at Syracuse last fall I was treated like family. Floyd's wife, DeBorah, was especially kind and generous with her time.

I think perhaps the most palpable thing you'll gain from *Floyd Little's Tales from the Broncos Sideline* is Floyd's passion. He had it as a player and, if anything, it's grown stronger as he continues to take time to influence the lives of everyone he meets.

A big reason Floyd agreed to do this book was because he wanted to talk about the forgotten Broncos heroes of his era. He felt it was important for younger fans to know that despite the losing records those Broncos teams from the 1960s and '70s, were a hardworking, dedicated group of professionals who loved the game and proudly played for the greatest fans in the world. Their unwavering commitment positively impacted the franchise's future, allowing today's Broncos to flourish as one of the marquee clubs in the NFL.

I could go on about Floyd. But by now, you've already seen for yourself that Floyd Little is not only a master storyteller, he's a truly an uncommon man.

–Tom Mackie

Celebrate the Heroes of Professional Football
in These Other NEW and Recent Releases from Sports Publishing!